AN EVERYDAY
GUIDE
TO
SCRIVENER 3
FOR
MAC

MARY CRAWFORD

Diversity Ink Press
Mary Crawford
www.MaryCrawfordAuthor.com

ISBN: 978-1-945637-57-5
ASIN: B07YSYWDZJ

Published October 28, 2019
by
Diversity Ink Press & Mary Crawford
Author may be reached at:
MaryCrawfordAuthor.com

Printed in The United States of America

To David Lee Martin who gave me the courage to start using Scrivener and Bobby Treat who frequently bails me out of trouble when I get stuck.

I am a more productive writer because you take the time to help me learn.

Table of Contents

Table of Figures

Chapter 1 –
Why Scrivener 3 for Mac?

If you're an author, your words have to go somewhere. One of the most heated debates in author communities is which program is best suited for writing books. There are passionate defenders of nearly every software and writing app. I won't lie, this book and my upcoming companion book, *An Everyday Guide to Scrivener 3 for Windows*, are unabashed love letters to the makers of Scrivener. This software has changed my writing life! My goal with this book is to help you become so comfortable with Scrivener 3 for Mac that using it becomes as natural as the programs you grew up using.

You don't have to take my word for it. Literature and Latte (the makers of Scrivener and Scrapple) offer a thirty-day free trial of their software for you to evaluate. This is not a stripped-down version which lacks features. They allow you to test the program as if you have paid for the application in full. The trial is for thirty days of use. Those days need not be consecutive. If you use the software every other day, it will last a couple of months. I am convinced that it won't take you that long to realize the benefits of Scrivener 3 for Mac.

Along the way, I will highlight important concepts I believe are especially helpful. The tips I share will be depicted as follows:

 Features tips related directly to a specific feature in Scrivener 3 for Mac.

 General tips designed to help you become a Scrivener 3 power user.

 Cautions against potential pitfalls or problems.

Helpful notes to highlight information.

Additionally, the following icons are used to explain keyboard shortcuts.

CHART KEY:
- ⌘ = Command Key (Apple Key)
- ^ = Control Key
- ⌫ = Delete Key
- ↓ = Down Arrow Key
- ⏎ = Return Key
- ← = Left Arrow Key
- ⌥ = Option Key (Alt Key)
- → = Right Arrow Key
- ⇧ = Shift Key
- ⇥ = Tab Key
- ↑ = Up Arrow Key

Let me say a bit about what this book is *not*. I am not a computer programmer. I am a former lawyer who discovered a passion for writing. This book is intended to give you practical tips on how to make Scrivener 3 work for you. It is not an exhaustive treatise on Scrivener 3, and it is not meant to be a programming manual.

I may not be computer savvy, but I am an enthusiastic fan of Scrivener 3. I'm excited to share my triumphs and failures with Scrivener 3 and how it has helped my writing career immensely.

My Personal Success Story

Those of you who follow me on social media or are part of the writing communities where I am active, probably know the story of how I became an author. It was never my goal, and no one is more surprised than me. I am a civil rights attorney by training and spent many years (before becoming an attorney) as a social service worker. A long time ago, an English teacher informed me I was the worst student he had ever had the displeasure of teaching. I believed him for decades until an author I was assisting told me she thought I had what it took to write great books.

Since health concerns made it impossible for me to work outside the home, I had nothing to lose. So, in November 2013, I started writing my first book. I was greener than green. I knew nothing about writing software, style guides, or beats. I just opened a Microsoft Word document and began telling a story.

It didn't take long for me to discover that I had a hard time keeping track of the story and everything else I needed at my fingertips. About three quarters of the way through Until the Stars Fall from the Sky, someone introduced me to Scrivener. It changed the way I write. I know that sounds like an overly dramatic declaration, but it's true. It's hard to underestimate the effect this one piece of software has had on the way I create books. Long story short, my first book was published in June 2014 and I have over thirty books published as I am writing this.

Thanks to Scrivener, my books are more organized, more consistent and better written than they would've been without this tool. I can manage my manuscript, keep my research in one location and refer to it often as I write. I can keep track of how many revisions I've done, and which chapters still need work. Finally, I can output the document however I wish. The flexibility is phenomenal. I don't know how I survived before Scrivener. I only wish I would've had this software when I was going through law school. It would've been amazingly helpful.

Perceptions of Scrivener

Like many of you, I heard that Scrivener is impossible to learn and so complex that you need a computer science degree to make it work. I'm here to tell you that's not true. I am not a computer programmer. My degrees are in Psychology and Jurisprudence. Yet, I am remarkably productive with Scrivener 3. I publish an average of seven books each year.

Initially, I was reluctant to even give the software a shot because who has time to learn a new software program when you're in the middle of writing books?

People told me learning Scrivener takes months and months because it's so complicated. Fortunately, that was not my experience. With the help of some video tutorials by David L. Martin, I was fully functional with Scrivener in just an afternoon or two. Did I mention I made the switch from Windows to Mac during the middle of National Novel Writing Month? Even so, I successfully completed NaNoWriMo and I've never looked back.

So, why does Scrivener 3 get such a bad rap? I'm not sure. I think a lot of it has to do with the fact that Scrivener is unlike any other software program I have encountered. It is completely adaptable to your style of writing. Consequently, the makers of Scrivener have built-in many layers of redundancy.

 If it's not comfortable for you to perform a task one way, there are probably three or four other ways to get the same job done.

Therefore, it's often difficult for people to ask questions about how to use the program. If they do, they're likely to get half a dozen different answers.

This is not a flaw.

It's the way the program is designed. The makers didn't want to confine Scrivener users to only one approach.

However, the program can seem overwhelming. It is my goal to help you identify the features which you will find most useful, while giving you a few tips and tricks to make writing books less painful.

Key Features of Scrivener 3

Sometimes, I wax poetically about the features of Scrivener 3. It's just that good. Initially, voice recognition software drew me to Scrivener 3. For those of you who don't use Dragon®, you might not know that it is painfully slow when you combine it with Microsoft Word. Even though Dragon® is compatible with Microsoft Word, they don't play very well together. So, I went searching for another option. That search eventually brought me to Scrivener 3 for Mac. I started out on the Windows version, but I wanted to have the features which are exclusive to Mac.

When my computer had a meltdown in the middle of NaNoWriMo, it was the perfect opportunity for me to make the switch to the Mac platform. I had never touched a Mac computer before that time, but it didn't take me long to fall in love with the comprehensive features in Scrivener for Mac. Of course, that was a while ago. I have upgraded twice, and I can't say enough nice things about the new features of Scrivener 3 for Mac. This program enables me to have a productive writing career.

My primary goal in switching platforms was to dictate directly into Scrivener 3 without having to copy and paste into a clipboard first. I find when I have to copy and paste, it interferes with my creative process. Therefore, I was ecstatic when I discovered that I could dictate directly into Scrivener 3 without having to do any additional data manipulation. Dragon® Professional Individual 6.0.8 works beautifully with Scrivener 3. It is fast and nimble.

Aside from my aversion to copying and pasting, there are many other features within Scrivener which makes it stand out over other writing applications.

First, it is eminently flexible. You can use this tool however you like.

If you already have a document you created elsewhere and you want to transfer it to Scrivener, you're covered. Scrivener has a tool for that.

If you want to write in an environment which has no distractions and a handy typewriter scrolling tool, no worries. Scrivener does that too.

Want to be able to track the dialogue of a specific character? Not a problem.

Do you need to analyze how often you use a specific word? Well, Scrivener has a tool for that too.

Do you need your manuscript to be available in multiple formats? That's no sweat for Scrivener. It is the easiest way I know to create multiple file types including .DOCX, .PDF, .EPUB, .MOBI, or .RTF files. One of the strengths of Scrivener 3 is that the output method doesn't change your core manuscript. Let's say you enter an esoteric literary contest which requires you to enter every other chapter. You can easily do so without having to copy and paste or do any other complicated gyrations with your words.

Making .MOBI or .EPUB files to upload to your favorite online retailer can be done with just a few clicks. A lot of authors are fans of Vellum software for formatting. However, I prefer the flexibility of Scrivener. I format all of my paperbacks and e-books with Scrivener.

One of my favorite features about Scrivener is its ability to keep everything organized in a system which makes sense. When I started writing, I tried to use a physical notebook for this task. I soon found frustrating limitations with this method. For example, if I need to reference pictures to describe a location or character, it's expensive to print them out. If I need to do research on a disability or medical issue, I often refer to several websites and medical journals to make sure my information is factually correct. By the end of a project, I can have dozens of these sites bookmarked. It got confusing to keep track of them all. If I print them out to put them in a notebook, I can't use search terms to find specific information. Scrivener allows me to collect websites, audio clips, movie clips, spreadsheets or external documents in one central location. I can organize these resources into folders so I'm able to easily locate the specific resource I need.

Scrivener offers help in world building too. If you're struggling to name your characters, Scrivener has a built-in name generator. You can even upload custom name vocabularies if you are working with a specific region or timeframe.

Character sheets are helpful in keeping track of your characters and what makes them unique. Scrivener comes with a built-in description template which allows you to track the physical, emotional and motivational features of each character.

Place sheets allow you to consistently describe locations. This can apply to countries, towns, or the local coffee shop. Speaking from personal experience, when you write over a series, it is critically important to keep the details consistent.

After you've written your manuscript, Scrivener has many tools to help make sure you produce your best work.

You can use the Snapshot and revision mode to keep track of changes to your manuscript. Additionally, Scrivener has great tools for cleaning up your novel. You can format all of your quotation marks however you wish and take care of any stray tab marks or unneeded returns.

For those of you who are interested in writing screenplays, Scrivener has a separate mode for scriptwriting. There is special pre-formatting available when you write in this mode.

Much to my delight, Scrivener has introduced a choice between light mode and dark mode. Headache sufferers like myself can rejoice! To access light and dark mode, you can either change your system preferences on your Mac or go to Appearance under the word Scrivener. Of course, you can always customize all the colors in Scrivener. I used to do this before the dark mode was created. Now, the new options simplify the process.

Honestly, this book was incredibly difficult to structure. Everything is so interrelated with Scrivener 3 it is difficult to explain one feature without presenting knowledge about another feature. Unfortunately, I can't tell you everything all at once. So, I had to pick an order to present the information.

 Feel free to skip around, using the table of contents or the index to find the specific information you need.

There are too many features in Scrivener to summarize in one chapter. So, I'll describe each of the moving parts in Scrivener one at a time so you can get a feel for how they work together. I'll start with choosing a template for your project.

Chapter 2 – The Moving Parts

Before I address individual parts of Scrivener, let me give an overview which might help you better understand how Scrivener works. When new users encounter Scrivener for the first time, they are often overwhelmed by the sheer number of options. This confusion is often compounded by the fact that there are several ways to accomplish the same thing in Scrivener. You can customize your workflow based on your preferences. Many things you can do in Scrivener can be done multiple ways.

I think it helps to view Scrivener as a collection of different software programs, instead of one program. I'm showing my age here, but I like to equate Scrivener to a Trapper Keeper. When I was

After I've done this, I use the Project Replace feature to change the default character names to the ones I'm using in my current project. In the example below, you can tell I am a pantser – as in I write by the seat of my pants. All the files are empty and the only thing I know for sure about this project is the title and who my characters are. When I write nonfiction, I don't tend to outline.

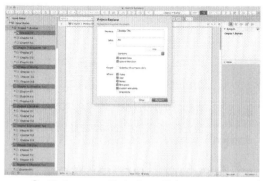

Figure 2: Using an Existing File as a Template

If your templates are smaller than mine, you can use the Save As Template function on the File menu. If you are able to do it this way, your custom template will appear when you set up a new file.

There are templates available on the Internet which can be imported into your Scrivener program. Use these with caution and virus check them first. Some of these files will cut down on your set up time. One of my favorites is *Romancing the Beat* by Gwen Haynes. Her template is available for free on her Internet site. If romance is not your thing, there are several others available for the

Snowflake Method, Save the Cat, and A Hero's Journey.

It's actually quite easy to import templates into Scrivener 3.

1. Open a new project.
2. Click on Options in the lower left-hand corner.
3. Click on Import Template.
4. Choose the template file from wherever you saved it.
5. You will be given the opportunity to categorize your template.
6. Your new template should now appear in whichever category you placed it in.

For example, I have imported a Snowflake Method template as well as a Romancing the Beat template. Although these templates can be helpful, if you wish, you can build your own novel by starting with a completely blank template.

In Scrivener 3, it is possible to have two documents open in the same window. This makes it easier to move back and forth between projects using tabs. Your documents will appear above the formatting bar. However, this feature also creates some difficulty if you want to drag folders from one project to another. If you have two documents open, you can click on Window ▸ Move Tab to New Window.

To make them appear as separate projects if you are moving back and forth between documents, it is helpful to click on Float Window. Float Window is also a helpful command if you are trying to drag things like your cover or websites into the research section of your Binder. Just remember to uncheck this option when you are finished. Otherwise, your project may not show up when you next click on Scrivener.

Where to Save Your File

If you are using Scrivener on different computers, you may want to use a cloud-based storage location to save your file. If you plan to use your project with the IOS version of Scrivener, you will need access to Dropbox.

How you save your project can help protect it from data loss. For some reason, if you use save as frequently, rather than save, there can be issues with data integrity. Unless you need to duplicate your file, I don't recommend using Save As.

Even though I don't use the IOS version a lot, I still save all my projects in the Scrivener file in my apps folder on Dropbox. There is a downside to this approach though. The IOS version requires lots of time to sync your files. So, if you have several of files in this folder, it could take a substantial amount of time before they are ready to use on your mobile device. If this is an issue, just move the Scrivener files you are not actively using to a different location.

Once you have chosen a template, now it's time to work with your project. To do this, it's helpful to know about the working parts of Scrivener 3. First, I'm going to talk about the Header Status Bar. I will refer to other key parts of Scrivener while I discuss the Header Status Bar, but don't worry I will fully explain each part later. The Header Status Bar is a very valuable tool for working with your manuscript.

The Header Status Bar

Right below the formatting bar, is a very helpful toolbar. I call it the Header Status Bar. This is a toolbar which changes its content depending upon which editing window you are in.

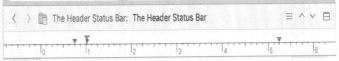

Figure 3: Header Status Bar in Scrivener 3

For example, if you are using the Document or Scrivenings mode, it contains the name of the folder you are currently using. The first two arrows on the right-hand side enable you to move between the last document you worked on and your current one.

On the right-hand side is an icon with three bars. If you click on that icon, it will show you the structure of your document (if it has sub-folders). This feature is particularly handy if you are working with a complex document with many levels in the Binder.

The up and down arrows move you between the documents in your section.

Lastly, there is a toggle switch for splitting your screen. You can split your screen vertically or horizontally. In Figure 4, I split my window to show one editor in Outline Mode and the other in Scrivenings mode.

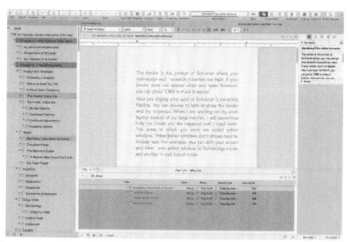

Figure 4: Split Window Containing Binder, Scrivenings , Outlining Mode, and the Inspector

If you click on the split window toggle while pressing the option key, you can change the orientation of your split panes from horizontal to vertical. When you are finished operating in split windows, just click on the icon again and you will go back to one window.

 When you are in split screen mode, the active window always has a blue status bar at the top of the window.

The blue status bar enables you to tell which window is active. I know this seems self-evident, but when you have several windows open, it can sometimes get confusing.

If you have your editing panes in different modes, make sure to choose which editing mode you want to be in before toggling back to one window.

The counterpart to the Header Status Bar is another dynamic toolbar I refer to as the Footer Status Bar.

The Footer Status Bar

At the bottom of any Scrivener project, there is a dynamic footer bar. Its contents change based on which mode you are operating in. it is one of the most quietly powerful features in Scrivener. It's not flashy, but it contains many helpful settings.

This menu will also allow you to move or copy folders. You can even move your folders to another project. This is particularly helpful if you are using a story bible in a series. You can just select the folders in your Binder and copy them to a different project.

We'll talk about collections later in Chapter 6, but among other things, this is a particularly powerful tool for checking for consistency within your manuscript.

If you want to change your documents to a folder or your folder to a document, you can do so from this menu. From a practical standpoint, there is very little difference between a document and a folder in Scrivener 3. I prefer to work in folders because Scrivener 3 will show you the sub-folders if you click on the parent folder. If you do the same in a document, the sub-documents will not be shown. Additionally, the default separators are different in files and documents. This can negatively affect your automatically generated table of contents – unless you adjust the properties.

Bookmarks are a new feature in Scrivener 3, and you can add them from this menu. I will talk about bookmarks under the Inspector section of this chapter.

Corkboard Options

When working in Corkboard Mode, the next section of the Footer Status Bar looks very similar to what you just saw in the Binder options. However, these icons control the corkboard window. So, you can add new documents or folders.

If you click on the gear, there will be a variety of options similar to the ones available in the Binder option. You can add and delete documents (in this view, they appear as index cards) or move them to the trash. From this menu, you can also move or copy folders – even between projects.

The icon to the right of the gear is grayed out unless you're working in Corkboard Mode with another window open (such as split screen or if the copy holder is open). To use this tool, make sure your split screen or copy holder is open and then click on the folder you want to open in the other window. It defaults to whatever group mode you have selected for the split screen.

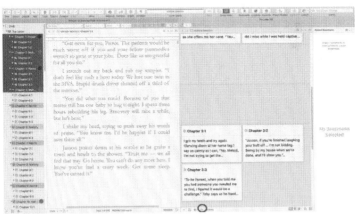

Figure 6: Automatic Selection in Spilt Screen

Honestly, before writing this book, I had never used that function before. I'm glad I discovered it because it solved one of the frustrations I have with using the corkboard. Sometimes, I want to see the sub-folders at the same time I look at the overall structure of my document. This tool allows that to happen.

Corkboard Appearance

The next section on the Footer Status Bar is an area in which you can change the appearance of your corkboard. You can have your index cards line up several ways and customize the size of the card and how many appear in a row. Scrivener has two main modes in the corkboard. One is a traditional view of your corkboard. The other allows you to move your files free-form and only commit them to your Binder when you choose. This is handy if you're moving around scenes and you're not exactly sure where you want them to go.

The last option is Arrange by Label. You can arrange your index cards to be presented vertically or horizontally. This feature is helpful if you are trying to track a particular point of view, timeline or location. You can toggle back and forth between the Arrange By Label or the traditional view.

One neat way to customize your index cards is to change the icon. Scrivener comes with many options, however you can also import your own custom icons into Scrivener. To do this, right-click on the folder in one of your index cards. Then, choose Change Icon and a menu will appear. At the very top of the menu is an option to Manage Custom Icons. There are many places where you can download icons for free or purchase a selection of them. Additionally, there are some available on the Literature and Latte site in this thread https://www.literatureandlatte.com/forum/viewtopic.php?f=18&t=17688.

Inspector Options

In the Inspector options, you can change the label type as well as the status.

Changing these options in the Inspector will change them in your Binder, Corkboard Mode and Outline Mode.

When you click on label, you'll be presented with a list of labels which already exist in your project. If you want to add or change options, scroll down to the bottom of this list to edit. You can edit both the label title and the color. Sometimes, if I am labeling to mark consistency, I will assign one character various shades of labels in a single color to help me visually track things.

The status options come pre-populated with some common choices like to-do, first draft, second draft, final draft, etc. However, you can add whatever you wish by clicking on edit. For example, I use a grammar checking program called ProWritingAid. So, after I run a chapter or section through the software program, I mark it as PWA cleared. After I listen to a chapter or scene (using the audio read back feature in the Mac operating system), I change the status to audio cleared. You can continue to change the status of your folders throughout the progress of writing your manuscript. Speaking from personal experience, there is nothing more satisfying than being able to change the status to **done**.

Binder

The Binder presents a clear and unambiguous representation of your project and is key to your project. You can use the Binder in different ways. Some authors write their books in one block without inserting chapters and scenes first. Others structure their manuscripts into chapters and subchapters. Still others use the Binder as a form of meticulous outline. Regardless of how you write, Scrivener has the flexibility you need.

The Binder has three mandatory types of folders and we will discuss the unique qualities of each one, and how they are used to pull together your manuscript.

Mandatory Files within Scrivener

The Binder is the portion of Scrivener where your manuscript and research materials are kept. If your Binder does not appear when you open Scrivener, you can press ⌥⌘B or click on the blue view icon in your toolbar to make it appear.

You can hide or show the Binder and the Inspector at any time.

Hiding the Inspector or Binder is as easy as clicking on the blue button in the toolbar which says View. Or you can elect to use the keyboard shortcut. You can hide the Binder by pressing ⌥⌘B, and the Inspector by using ⌥⌘I. When I am working on my small laptop instead of my large monitor, I sometimes hide the Binder and the Inspector until I need them. The areas in which you work are called editor windows. These editor windows don't always have to include only your Scrivenings. For example, you can split your screen and view one editor window in Scrivenings mode and another in Corkboard Mode.

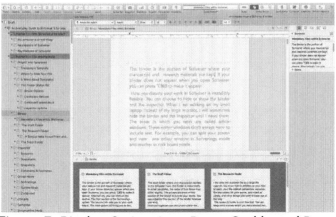

Figure 7: Binder, Scrivenings Pane, Corkboard Pane, and Inspector

The Binder contains three main sections: the Draft Folder, the Research Folder and the Trash Folder. These folders are mandatory in your Binder. In some templates, the names may vary. For example, if you use the screenplay template, the folder is called screenplay, not draft. Each mandatory folder has a unique purpose. You may rename them, but the function stays the same. For the program to function properly, these three types of files need to be in your Binder.

If the Binder is not showing in your project, you can toggle it on and off with the keyboard shortcut ⌥⌘B. Alternatively, you can show it under the View menu.

The first section in the Group Mode is the Scrivenings option. The second will take you to your corkboard. The third option will bring you to the outline view.

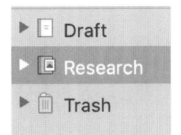

Figure 8: Three Mandatory Folders Within the Binder

You'll note that these folders have unique icons attached to them to denote their special status. Although you can rename these folders, you may not want to for the sake of clarity.

 If you click on the triangle icon beside the folder or document, it will expand sub-folders or sub-documents, if there are any. If you want to use a keyboard shortcut, click on the top level of the folder or document in the Binder you wish to examine and use the ^⌘ with the arrow keys. This works to move your folders or documents up and down your Binder.

The Draft Folder

The Draft Folder is where your manuscript resides. In the template I use, this folder is called draft. In other templates, the name of this folder may differ slightly. For example, some templates may call it a screenplay and others a manuscript. The primary purpose of this section of the Binder is to hold your words. You can organize this section of the Binder however you wish.

How you organize your manuscript within the Draft Folder is completely up to you. Personally, I write my books in chapters and scenes.

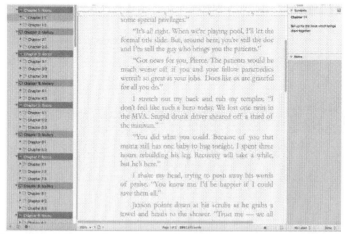

Figure 9: View of Binder with Subchapters, Scrivenings, and the Inspector

However, not everyone writes this way – and that's completely fine. Other authors prefer to write their text in one big block and separate it out later. Scrivener has a mechanism for automatically dividing your document into folders. We'll discuss that in Chapter 5.

 If you use voice recognition software with Scrivener 3 and your computer starts to lag, you may want to break up large blocks of text into smaller sections.

If you are a fan of extensively outlining, Scrivener is exceedingly well suited for your approach. You can nest folders as deeply as you need to. You can use folders or documents.

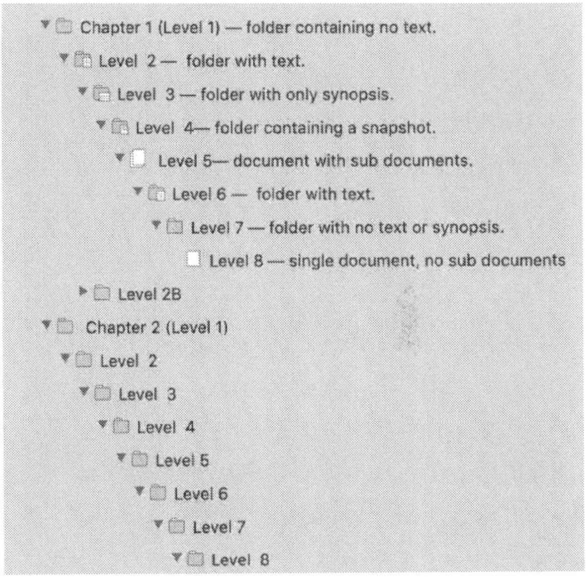

Figure 10: Different Levels of Folders in the Binder with Icon Types

Scrivener offers visual cues to help you determine what is in each folder. I have noted them above. For example, if you save a Snapshot in a folder, the folder looks different from the one with only a synopsis. This feature is handy when you are trying to determine where you are in your project.

To add folders or documents to your Binder, press on the green +. From there, you can choose whether you want to add a folder or a document. Alternatively, you can click on the + in the Footer

Status Bar if you want a document, or the file containing a + if you want a folder. You may also use keyboard shortcuts. ⌘N creates a new document and ⌘ ⌥N creates a new folder.

Incidentally, it makes little difference whether you use a folder or a file. For almost every purpose, they are the same in Scrivener. There are a couple of notable exceptions. If you use a document, your sub documents won't automatically be displayed in the Scrivenings pane, whereas the content will be displayed if you click on a folder with sub-folders. Additionally, files and documents have a different default scene separator. This is easily changed in the settings, but if you don't know about the variation, it can trip you up.

In addition to Styles which change the way your Scrivener document appears on the screen, Scrivener 3 has introduced Section Types. I will discuss more about these in Chapter 5. I mention them here because if you plan to compile your manuscript in the compiler, each folder or document will need to have a Section Type. You can right-click on any folder or document in your Binder and assign one. The same is true about labels and status.

If you don't already have the arrow tool in your toolbar, you may want to skip ahead to Chapter 3 to learn how to customize your toolbar to include this handy tool:

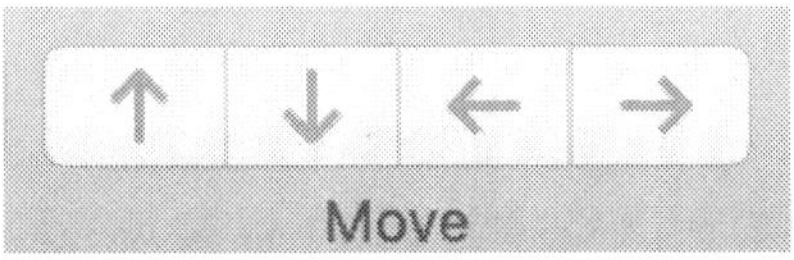

Figure 11: Toolbar Option to Move Folders in the Binder

These arrows help you determine where your files appear in the hierarchy under the Binder. Think of it as indenting levels in an outline. In fact, because of the way Scrivener operates, these files will appear in your outline with the level you have assigned to each folder or document. Hierarchy in your Binder can be important when automatically formatting your manuscript. Try to make sure your chapters and the subchapters have a consistent hierarchy within your Binder. It will make things easier later on.

If your Binder is collapsed, you can expand it by clicking on the expand and collapse buttons available in the toolbar or you can click on the arrow beside the icon in the folder. Additionally, you can use the arrow keys as navigation tools as long as you have clicked on the file first.

The Research Folder

I like to view the Research Folder as a large file cabinet. You know how in addition to your files at work, your file cabinet sometimes becomes the depository for your backpack, your stash of candy, and other things you want to keep out of the way?

The Research Folder is a bit like that. You can keep extra scenes which you have elected not to use in a folder in the research section of the Binder, or you can drag websites to this section so they are at your fingertips. Additionally, you can add your cover or other pictures of your characters to help ensure your descriptions are accurate. You can save movie or audio clips here too. Sometimes, these are essential for setting the mood or portraying an accent accurately. I keep information about story beats in this folder too.

 Your front and back matter files also go in the research section. Because they are in the research section, you can add pictures for your chapter headings or section art.

A Special Note About Front and Back Matter

Interestingly, your front and back matter files go in your Research Folder even though they may contain critical parts of your manuscript. Scrivener treats these files differently than others and there is a mechanism to compile front and back matter into your manuscript. Keeping the front and back matter sections separate from your manuscript ensures that your novel starts on page one, even when you have a dedication, acknowledgments, copyright information or a forward.

Files for the back matter work the same way as front matter folders. They are stored in the same location under the research portion of your Binder. You can have more than one option for back matter material. For example, you may want to include links to Amazon for your Kindle e-books and change those links to other sources when you go wide because retailers like Apple, Kobo and Barnes & Noble may not accept Amazon links.

If you use the novel template, Scrivener already has pre-made documents set up in the Binder to make the process easier.

Keeping your front and back matter separate makes it easier for you to update your manuscript as necessary.

I happen to use the same front matter regardless of whether I'm creating an e-book or a PDF or Word document for my paperbacks. Other authors elect to have separate ones.

Figure 12: Front Matter in Research Folder Within Binder

If your books are on multiple marketing platforms, you can have one set of front and back matter which refers people to Amazon sites and another copy of the back matter which is free of any offending links. This will allow you to upload your book to different platforms such as Apple, Kobo, and Barnes & Noble.

If you are like me and you tend to use the same front and back matter, you can drag the folders from one project to another (if you don't already have it built into your template).

I also keep a copy of my e-book cover in the front matter folder to make it easy to locate when I'm ready to compile. If I want to, I can bookmark this file in other chapters. This is handy if you need to describe your cover models in detail for a certain scene.

The Trash Folder

The Trash Folder is an important safety net. Don't empty it until you are 100% sure you will never need its contents. Once emptied, you can't retrieve what you've placed there.

The Trash Folder is just what it sounds like. It's where you throw parts of your document away. For example, in my template I use for my fiction novels,

I have three sections under each chapter. Sometimes, I don't divide each chapter into three sections so I toss the unneeded folders in the trash. I also throw away the files which contain my book lists when they become outdated. I just replace them with new ones.

What you put in the Trash Folder stays there until you empty the trash. Don't empty the trash unless you are 100% certain you will never need the information in the Trash Folder.

Fortunately for those of us who are prone to making mistakes, files you put in the trash can be easily dragged back up to your draft file and put back where they belong. (As long as you haven't emptied the trash.)

One additional note about the Trash Folder. I have noticed that sometimes when I use the Import and Split feature, the manuscript and all of its resulting chapters may inadvertently end up in the Trash Folder. If this happens to you, just collapse the files and drag your manuscript up to your Draft Folder.

 The keyboard shortcut to move an object into the trash is ⌘⌫.

To delete only portions of the trash, highlight the folders you wish to delete permanently and right-click. On the menu there will be an option to delete. Select delete. Use caution when choosing this option, as it permanently deletes your files.

Inspector

The Inspector is like the planner portion of the Trapper Keeper where you keep all your additional information to ensure your project goes smoothly. It's kind of a catchall tool for external information.

To access the Inspector, click on the blue I in the toolbar. Alternatively, you can use the keyboard shortcut which is ⌥⌘I to toggle the Inspector on or off. You can also access the setting under View.

Figure 13: Inspector Icon in Scrivener 3 for Mac

Synopsis

Simply put, the synopsis is an area in which you can describe the chapter or section you're working on. This information can also appear in the outline. If you change the name in this window, it will also change in your Binder and in the outline. Every document or file will have its own synopsis.

If you have more than one file selected in your binder, your synopsis will not show. Instead, you will be presented with the bookmark tab.

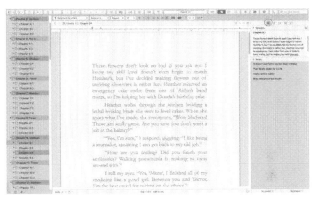

Figure 14: The Synopsis Within the Inspector Pane

In the example above, I have used the Auto Fill tool under Documents to automatically fill in the text under the chapter title. This tool populates the synopsis from the text you have written in your Scrivenings. Alternatively, you can place your main plot points in this area. Your synopsis will also appear on your index cards in the corkboard view. It is possible to add a picture to your synopsis. To add a picture to your synopsis, click on the picture in the upper right-hand corner then drag an image to the Inspector. You can toggle back and forth between your picture or the written synopsis.

Place a picture of your characters in the synopsis to enable you to describe them more accurately.

The synopsis tab in the Inspector also has a place for notes. I will often use this area to reinforce the story beats I want to hit in a particular chapter. After I've written my manuscript, I use this area to note any typos my beta readers found after editing.

Bookmarks

In a substantial upgrade to previous versions, Scrivener consolidated and replaced References, Project Notes and Favorites with Bookmarks.

Although it looks innocuous in the Inspector, Bookmarks are a very powerful feature.

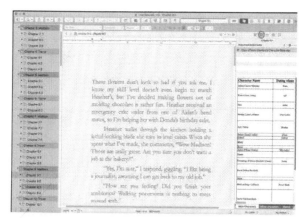

Figure 15:Bookmarks Within the Inspector Pane

In the example above, the bookmark section includes my character bible. Because I used the click and drag feature to place a link to my Excel spreadsheet into the bookmark area, I am able to click on the character bible and edit the original file. This technique works phenomenally well if you are working with an external outlining or timeline program like Aeon or Scrapple.

But that's not all the bookmarks can do. This new feature allows you to drag existing folders from your Binder to the bookmarks. This is helpful if you are working with character sheets or need to have specific details from a chapter available with just a click.

 You can save a bookmark as either a document bookmark or a project bookmark by clicking on the up and down arrow next to the gear. If you designate a bookmark as a project bookmark, it will be available for every file or document in your binder. This is very helpful for links to story bibles.

In addition to files from your Scrivener project, you can link to documents, websites, Excel files, databases, or calendars. Virtually anything you can drag into the bookmark area becomes a live, dynamic resource.

It is possible to add multiple resources into the same bookmarking section. You just need to click and drag. To accomplish this, simply open Finder and locate the file you want to use (if it's not already in your Scrivener project) and drag it to the top section of the bookmark. To bookmark particular sections of your Binder, just drag the folder over into the bookmark section you want to work with.

Metadata

The Metadata is a very helpful part of the Inspector. This tab looks a little like a price tag and it's between the bookmark and the Snapshot.

First, it allows you to see when a document or folder was created and the last time you modified it.

Next, you can check a box to include this folder or document in your compile settings. So, if you write a document you don't want in your final output, just uncheck this box.

You can also assign section layouts. There will be a dropdown list of available section layouts or you can add one of your own. I will discuss section layouts in detail in Chapter 5.

Custom Metadata allows you to track specific data through each folder or document. For example, when I'm writing a book which contains a secret which some characters know and others do not, I use Metadata to tell me which chapters discuss the big secret. You could also use this tool to track point of view, location or events on a timeline. You can elect to show your custom Metadata in Outline Mode.

You can add keywords to the next section. Keywords can appear in your outline or on the edge of your index cards. You can add keywords to track plots and subplots, time and location, the presence of certain characters in your document or folder. If you have a novel which changes tense, you might want to use keywords to indicate the switch. To add a new keyword, click on the +. If you want to delete a keyword you've already added, just use the subtract sign. You can click on the gear to show existing keywords or to add new ones.

Snapshot

Snapshot is one of the most overlooked features in Scrivener. As authors, we tend to edit our work a lot. Using Snapshot is an excellent way to keep track of your changes and compare them.

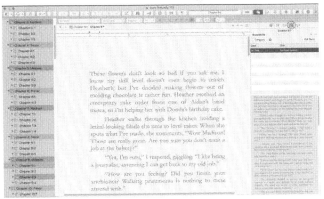

Figure 16: Snapshot Within the Inspector Pane

Let's say you're not certain which direction you want to go with a character and you want to try out an alternative storyline. No problem! Scrivener has you covered with Snapshot.

Snapshot are a way for Scrivener to remember what you've just written and keep a copy – even when you write over the original manuscript with new information. If you don't like the changes you make, you can roll back to the version saved in your Snapshot. It is possible to have multiple Snapshot of a single file within your Binder. That's why it's a good idea to give each one a unique title. The Snapshot Manger can be accessed by clicking Documents ‣ Snapshots ‣ Show Snapshot Manger. By clicking on the gear next to the Compare Button, you can choose to compare differences in your snapshots by paragraph, clause, or word.

You can place an icon in your toolbar which will allow you to save titled Snapshot with just a click. Alternatively, Snapshot is the first menu item under documents.

If I were to identify one feature in Scrivener I don't use nearly enough, it would be Snapshot. Honestly, I forget the feature is available until after I've made changes and think to myself I should've taken a Snapshot of that. So, if you are new to Scrivener 3, it's a good idea to get in the habit of taking Snapshot as you go along.

You can choose multiple files in your Binder to include in your Snapshot by pressing down on the ⌘ while you click on individual folders or documents in your Binder.

Comments & Footnotes

The last section in the Inspector pane is the comments section. By highlighting a sentence or phrase and adding a comment, you can easily find it later to make edits or corrections. If you like to follow an outline, I recommend using the comment feature to identify areas in which your characters decided to deviate from your carefully plotted ideas. This will help you identify areas which may lack cohesion in your final manuscript.

After you've addressed the issues you identify with comments, they can be deleted.

The comment icon looks like a speech bubble. Next to it, there are two small letters CF.

If you have your cursor in your Scrivenings window, you can click on these letters and add a footnote.

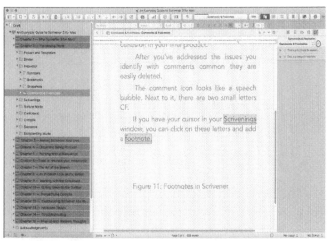

Figure 17: Footnotes in Scrivener

It's pretty easy to see where your footnotes are in Scrivener. You can change how your footnotes appear in Preferences (⌘,) under editing.

This is how the above section looks when it is compiled into a Word document.

Figure 18: Footnotes from Scrivener Displayed in a Word Document

I'm aware that not everyone writes novels. That's okay. Scrivener has several templates for different types of work including academic projects and they provide more direct guidance on using footnotes than the novel templates.

It is easy to identify which sections have comments or footnotes in the Inspector. There will be a dot beside the comment tab if your folder or document contains footnotes or comments.

Removing a comment or footnote is as easy as clicking the subtract sign in the Inspector.

Scrivener also allows you to export your comments and footnotes to an external file. This is helpful if you are working with an external reference manager program.

Group Mode

The group mode refers to the way you view your manuscript in Scrivener. There are three views included in the group mode. The first is the Document or Scrivenings Mode, which is represented by two pieces of paper. Document Mode is also referred to as Scrivenings Mode because it displays more than one file if selected in the binder. The second view is the Corkboard Mode. If you squint, you can envision its icon as representing index cards on a corkboard. The third view is the Outlining Mode. It is represented by blue lines of different shades. Abstractly, it looks like an outline. This group mode appears by default on your toolbar. The mode you have selected will be highlighted. In this case, I am in the Document Mode. You can also use keyboard shortcuts to get to each view in group mode. The Scrivenings mode can be accessed by pushing ⌘1. If you wish to be in Corkboard Mode, press ⌘2. To switch to Outline Mode, use ⌘3.

Figure 19: Group Mode in Scrivener 3

If you have your Binder and your Inspector open, the middle pane is referred to as the editor window. This window has a different appearance depending upon which group mode you are operating in. You can have changes made in your corkboard appear in your Binder. Alternatively, if you just want to experiment with the Corkboard without impacting your Binder, you do not have to commit the changes to the Binder. I will discuss the functions included in the Corkboard more in Chapter 10.

Scrivenings

I'll admit, when I first was watching tutorials about Scrivener, I was confused about the term Scrivenings. It's actually a rather exotic term used to describe the portion of Scrivener which looks like a word processor. This is also referred to as Document Mode. Unfortunately, this mode is referred to differently in different parts of Scrivener 3 for Windows documentation and file menus.

You can write directly in the Document Mode and do all the typical things you would usually do in a word processing program. You can format your words as bold, italic or underline. You can change the justification, color, and line spacing.

The line spacing function looks a little different from other word processing programs. However, it's pretty straightforward.

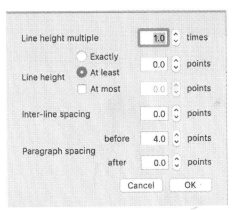

Figure 20: Line Spacing in Scrivener 3

In the Scrivenings window, if you have a document with several sub documents, they will be displayed with section dividers on the screen. Most commonly, this is displayed as a dashed line. However, you can easily change the default setting.

The appearance of this divider can be changed under Preferences (⌘,). The setting is found under the general tab.

The Document or Scrivenings Mode is one of many places you can assign Scrivener's new style feature. Styles are the way you tell Scrivener how you want your words to appear. This includes things like font choice, spacing, special formatting like small caps and justification. I will be discussing them in greater detail in chapter 5.

You can also change the font or font size in the Scrivenings page without applying a style.

If you choose N/A when you are compiling, Scrivener will use your default settings to determine the appearance of each folder or document.

When you are producing e-books, indenting using tabs or manual spacing is problematic. It is preferable to use the ruler to set your margins and indents.

Using the Ruler

Tabs and manual spacing don't work particularly well when producing e-books.

Scrivener's solution to this is the ruler.

The ruler allows you to set indents and margins without using tabs.

To make the ruler appear, either place an icon for it on your toolbar or press ⌘R. If you have a ruler with complex settings, and you want to move the settings from project to project, there is a mechanism to copy and paste your ruler by using ^⌘C for copy and ^⌘V for paste.

 Unlike some word processors, the ruler in Scrivener 3 starts at zero. This setting is calibrated to where your text starts, not to the edge of the paper. You will need to adjust your margins accordingly.

Figure 21: Ruler with Margins and Indent Shown

To set an indent, drag the T at the top of the ruler to the depth you would like your paragraphs to be indented. The same concept applies to setting your margins. Just drag the triangles from either end to the measurements you prefer.

 Using the ruler to set your margins and indents makes it easier to format your book.

Outline Mode

One of Scrivener's three group modes is the Outlining Mode. As with other areas of Scrivener, usually if you change the title of one of the folders or documents in your outline, it will appear on the cards in the Corkboard Mode and in your Binder. For the outline feature to work properly, you need to select a folder in your Binder which has some documents.

To make the Outline Mode appear, click on the icon in your toolbar with the blue lines or press ⌘3. You can expand or collapse your outline by using ⌘9 and ⌘0, or by clicking the expand and collapse icons in your toolbar if you have customized it to include them.

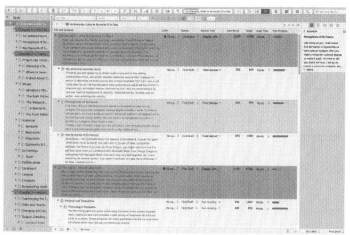

Figure 22: Outline Pane with Synopsis Showing

As you can see in the figure above, I have the outline displayed with the synopsis information that was automatically generated from my text. You can toggle the synopsis on and off by clicking on the button at the bottom of the screen on the right-hand side. Additionally, you can choose which information to display in your Outline Mode by clicking on the button which looks like a ▸ on the top right-hand side of the window. This symbol appears right next to the Inspector if you are displaying the Inspector window. Choose which options you want to display in the Outline Mode. In Figure 22, I have added columns for targets, word counts and progress.

One of the new features introduced in Scrivener 3 allows you to change your styles from the outline pane. Sometimes, it's easier to see which format to use when you can get an overview of your whole document. Changing the styles in the outline pane also changes them in the Binder and the corkboard pane. This is also true if you add more files or change the synopsis information while in the outline pane.

You can work with your manuscript in the outline pane, just like you would if you were writing an outline on paper. To add a new folder, just click on the folder with the + in the lower left-hand corner located on the footer toolbar.

You can press ⌘N for a new document or ⌘⌥N for a new folder. This shortcut works in the Binder, Corkboard Mode or Outline Mode.

You can move folders within your outline with either the arrow buttons in your toolbar or by pressing ^⌘→ or ^⌘←. However, there is a limit to the number of levels you can move using the keyboard shortcuts. If you've reached this limit, the folders or documents will not move.

I will discuss more advanced features of the Outline Mode in Chapter 11.

The Corkboard Mode is another view within group mode which lets you see in different levels. Some authors prefer to work with index cards and sticky notes. The corkboard has many helpful features to move your planning to the digital world.

Corkboard

If you are a fan of working with index cards or sticky notes to organize (or reorganize) your manuscript, the Corkboard Mode might be for you. This feature in Scrivener is exactly what it sounds like. It is a mode which allows you to view your manuscript in electronic index cards. If you wish, you can even change the background of your index cards so they resemble traditional cards.

Although the Outline Mode and Corkboard Mode present your manuscript in different formats, many of the keyboard shortcuts that are applicable to the outline pane are the same in the corkboard pane.

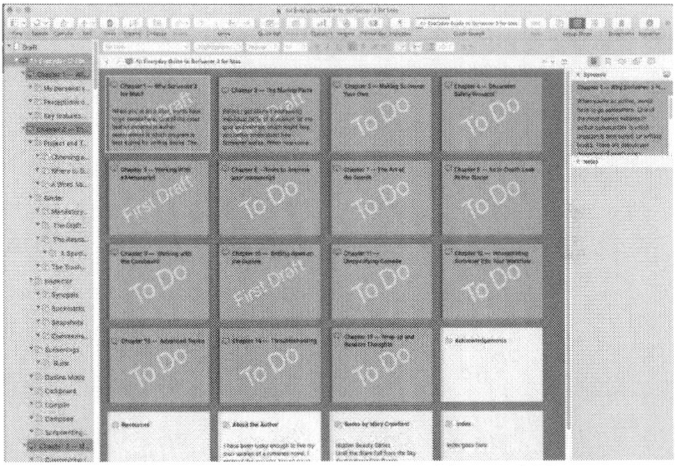

Figure 23: Scrivener in Corkboard View

To enter the Corkboard Mode, click on the orange box with four white squares in the group mode on the toolbar (or press ⌘2). It is important to remember that you need to be in a folder with sub-folders for this feature to work properly. I usually work from the folder which contains all my other folders when I work in Corkboard Mode so I can see the whole of my document. The colors I use in my labels determine the colors of the index cards. You can turn off this feature. The stamps are determined by the status I assigned each section on the footer bar. You can toggle the stamp feature on and off with ^⌘S. You can also choose the opacity of the stamp under Preferences (⌘,).

See the stacks with multiple cards? That indicates it is a folder or document with sub-folders or some documents. To get to the sub-folders, click on the folder on the index card. Doing this will open up the sub-folders or sub documents.

In Scrivener 3, there is a new view for the corkboard pane. You can elect to show your cards in a new format called Arrange By Label. There is an option to switch between vertical and horizontal. This feature can be handy when tracking time, location or points of view. In the example below, my story has several points of view. So, I can see where each index card appears in relation to other points of view. You can toggle back and forth between the traditional view and Arrange by Label without affecting your manuscript.

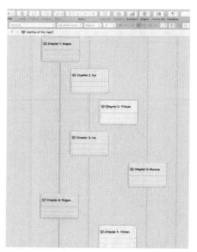

Figure 24: Corkboard Arrange By Label View

In Arrange By Label view, changing the label of your folder or document is as simple as dragging it to another label color on the corkboard.

The corkboard also has several modes for manipulating index cards (other than arrange by label). One is a traditional arrangement of your index cards. In this mode, if you make changes to the order of your index cards, the order of files in your Binder and outline also change. However, you can elect to go into free-form view. If you are in this view, the changes you make in the corkboard don't appear in your Binder or outline until you click the commit button. This feature is incredibly helpful when you are moving around scenes and chapters to see where they fit the best. You can experiment without affecting your Binder or outline. When your index cards are to your liking, you can click on the commit button. Your binder and outline will be rearranged accordingly.

After you've worked with your manuscript in one of the group modes, you probably want to compile your results. Although it seems like a scary term, compile is just the name Literature and Latte has given the process of collecting all of your individual documents and creating a cohesive document for use in Microsoft Word, PDF, or e-book (among many other formats). I'll give an overview of the Compile function next.

Compile

Of all the features in Scrivener 3, the most changed from the prior version is the compiler (⌥⌘E). For those of you who are new to Scrivener, compile is the way you tell Scrivener to put together the parts of your manuscript. This is one of the hardest concepts for many users of Scrivener to grasp.

 The compile feature allows you to change the appearance of your output without having to physically change your manuscript.

 One of the primary benefits to using the compile feature is that you can output your manuscript as several file types such as .PDF, .EPUB, .MOBI, or .DOCX without having to use an external program.

Learning to compile will save you copious amounts of time. I will discuss Compile in depth in Chapter 11, but I will give a brief description and overview here.

I understand the compile feature looks hopelessly complicated. When I first used it, I'd never seen anything like it, and I struggled to understand the concept. Hopefully, I can simplify it for you so it is not so intimidating. To open the compile feature, click on your toolbar or press ⌥⌘E.

As you can see in the figures below, your compile pane can look different depending on the type of file you are creating, the format you choose and which section layouts you include. For example, the top window contains the settings I use when I write nonfiction. The next figure shows my custom format that I've developed for my fiction novels. In this case, it is showing the options for my Hidden Beauty Series.

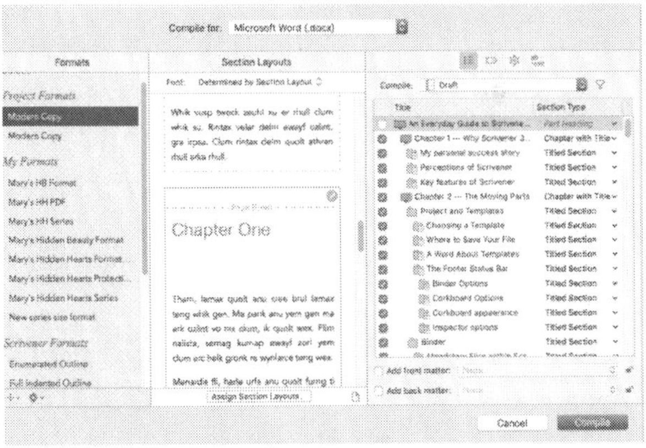

Figure 25: Compile Window In Scrivener 3

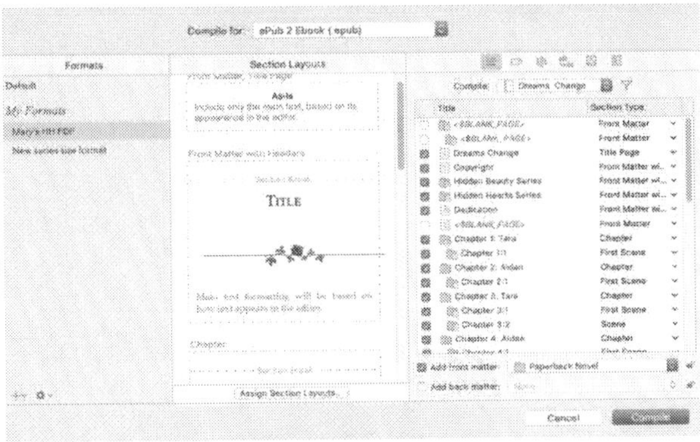

Figure 26: Custom Format in the Compile Window in Scrivener 3

On the surface, the Compiler looks incredibly different from earlier versions. However, many parts of it function the same way as it used to. There are four main parts to the compiler menu. At the very top, you choose which type of output you would like to create.

At the top of the menu, you choose the output of your manuscript. I most commonly use Microsoft .DOCX or EPUB 2. However, there are more than a dozen output options to choose from.

The options in the left-hand side of the window under format change depending on which output method you chose. The formats provided by Scrivener have pre-populated options in them based on their function. You can always change a Scrivener format to customize it to your needs. Formats can be saved to each individual project or globally.

 If you want to share your Scrivener file with someone else, and you want them to be able to see exactly how you formatted it, you need to save your format as a Project Format instead of under My Formats.

On the right-hand side of the Compiler Window is the list of folders or documents in your project. You simply check the ones you want to have included in your output.

If you want to select all the files in the Compile Pane press ⌥ while you click in the checkbox.

All of your documents in this window will have a Section Type attached. If the wrong Section Type appears, click on the down arrow and choose another Section Layout from the menu. If for some reason your manuscript is not compiling correctly, this is one place to look for mistakes.

In Figure 26, I am compiling an .EPUB file, so I don't need any blank pages like I do when I am formatting a paperback. Therefore, I unchecked those boxes.

There are other options in this pane which I will discuss later in Chapter 11.

In Scrivener 3, the middle pane is new. In this window, you assign section formats to your project format.

The compile function in Scrivener 3 is phenomenally flexible. You can customize your formats to include several types of fonts, graphics, font effects, line spacing, or colors. This is accomplished through the application of different Section Types. This process is slightly different from earlier versions of Scrivener and it takes a bit of time to set up. However, the good news is once you set up the format and assign Section Types, you can use them over and over again.

When you choose a different type of output, the available format options change. For example, you will have different formats available if you choose .EPUB for an e-book or a Microsoft document or .PDF for paperback.

 I recommend exporting your formats and saving them in a safe place like an USB drive in case your favorite format gets corrupted.

I've had this happen before. Fortunately, I had exported my formats and was able to delete the corrupt one and use the working one.

Remember when I was discussing the Scrivenings window? I briefly discussed applying Section Layouts to each folder or document. The compiler is where it all comes together.

In the left-hand side of the window are the formats. This is how you tell Scrivener what you want your manuscript to look like. If you right-click on the Format, you can edit it.

 I recommend that you duplicate the format before you edit it. If you choose Duplicate Format, you will be given the opportunity to save it.

You can either save it as a Project Format, which attaches it only to the particular project you are working on, or you can save it to my formats which makes it globally available.

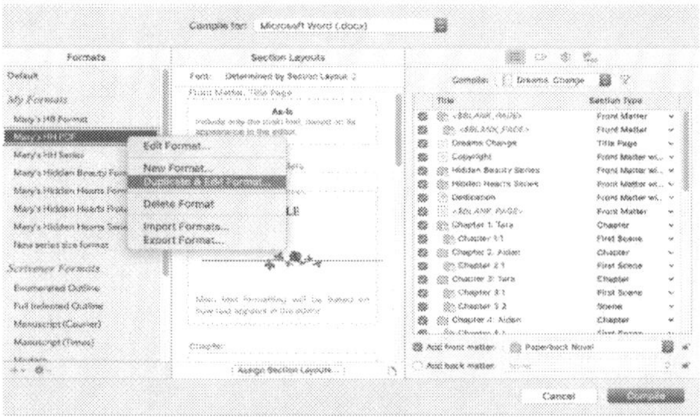

Figure 27: Editing Formats in Compile Window

Clicking on Edit Format or Duplicate and Edit brings you to a window that you might recognize from Scrivener 2. Your Section Layouts are listed in this window. You can add or subtract different types of Section Layouts here. You need to set your preferences for each type of Section Layout you plan to use. In this particular project, I am only using five of the six different section layouts available in this format. They are indicated in bold.

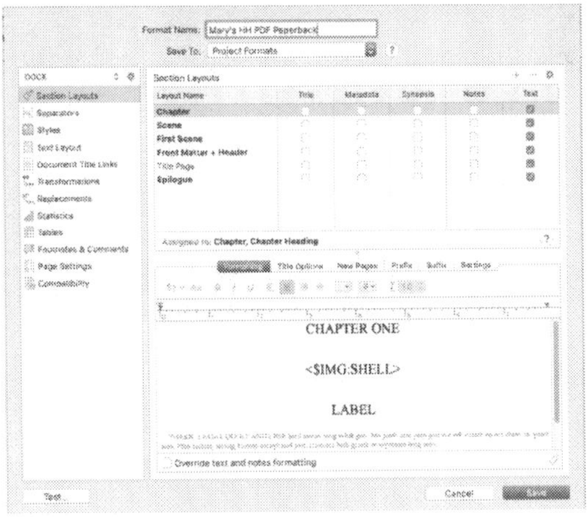

Figure 28: Editing Format Options in Scrivener 3

You can make changes to several Section Layouts in this window. However, make sure to click save when you're done.

If you create a new Section Type while you are in compile, in order for the system to work properly, you need to add it to the Section Layout menu. To do this, simply right click on one of your folders and go down to Edit. When you click Edit, a window listing all of your Section Types will appear. Just click the plus sign and add the title of your section. Although, the names do not need to be identical; it helps improve clarity if you name them something similar.

From this menu, you can also add new labels or status types as well as things you want to track with Custom Metadata.

Section Types	Section Types Default Types by Structure
Label List	Section types are used by the current Compile format to determine how documents appear when compiled.
Status List	
Custom Metadata	Part Heading
Formatting	First Scene
Auto-Complete List	Title Page
Special Folders	Chapter Heading
Background Images	Scene
Backup	Chapter
	Epilogue
	Heading
	Section
	Front Matter
	Front Matter with Headers
	N/A

+ −

Cancel   OK

Figure 29: Section Layout Menu in Scrivener 3

Scrivener 3 has a new feature which was not present in Scrivener 2. This is the middle pane where you assign layouts to your Format. Think of this as different parts of Scrivener shaking hands. You've already determined which Section Layout you want for each document or folder in your Binder, now assigning section formats will tell Scrivener which Section Layout goes with each specific option in your format.

If you haven't assigned your section layouts to a specific format, you will see a yellow warning label advising you to assign your layouts.

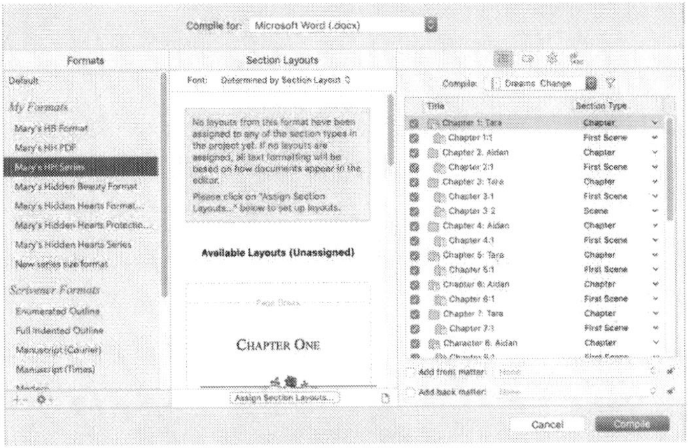

Figure 30: Assign Section Layout Warning

Once you click on Assign Section Layouts, Scrivener 3 will bring up a window like this:

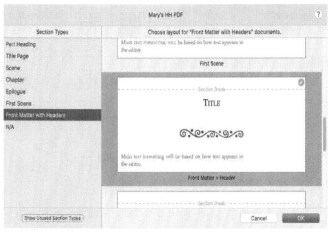

Figure 31: Assigning Layouts Within Scrivener 3

If you right-click on the options in the left-hand pane, it brings up a drop-down menu which makes it easy to choose which Section Layout you want to apply. Alternatively, you can just click on the style you want for each Section Type.

In Chapter 11, I will have a thorough discussion of all the features in Compile. This section is meant to be an overview to highlight the changes between older versions of Scrivener and the update to Scrivener 3.

One of the most popular features in Scrivener is its ability to block out all distractions while you write. In the next section, I will discuss the Compose Window.

Compose

Distraction is the bane of authors everywhere. Scrivener has a cure for that. It's called the Compose Mode. You can click on the composition button in the toolbar or use ⌥⌘F. This is a toggle command, but you can also use the escape key to get back to your normal view in Scrivener. You can also find this option under the view menu.

This mode has a very minimal display. However, if you need to do things like change the style of your document or assign a section layout, those options are available to you. Additionally, you can change the paper size and where it is presented on your screen. For me, this particular option is very helpful because I have cerebral palsy and I write from bed. My monitor isn't lined up perfectly within my line of sight. In composition mode, I can place the paper on the right-hand side of the monitor which makes it easier for me to see.

 My other favorite feature in composition mode is typewriter scrolling. It means no matter how much you type, your cursor will stay in the center of your paper. No more scrolling!

I find that I am more productive when I use this mode. Primarily, this is because I'm not reminded of the dozen other things I need to do on my computer while I am writing. On my wish list for the makers of Scrivener, Literature and Latte, is a timer in this mode for those of us who like to sprint. When I write in the compose mode, I use the timer on my phone instead of the one on the computer.

If you have a small picture (under 1 MB), you can change the settings under preferences to use your image as the background in this mode. I use covers of my books so that if I need to describe a facial feature or something it's right there in front of me.

The Go To menu will allow you to go anywhere in your Binder and the Inspector button will pull up your Inspector window if you need to consult your notes or other details about your folder or document. There is a word count visible on the toolbar. You can display this toolbar or automatically hide it. The choice is yours. This setting is also found in Preferences (⌘,).

If you prefer to limit your distractions while you write, in addition to the Compose Mode, Scrivener 3 has a Focus Mode. It is a tool which allows you to block out everything except for the single line, sentence, or paragraph are working on.

Focus Mode

In all honesty, Scrivener is so full of cool features, I didn't even know Focus Mode existed until I started writing this book. I frequently write in compose mode to block out distractions, but the focus mode lets you take that concept even further. In the focus mode, I am able to gray out everything else in my project window except for the line, sentence or paragraph I am currently working on. In order to set up the options in focus mode, click on View ▸ Text Editing ▸ Focus. You can have it focus on each line, sentence or paragraph.

I encountered one small anomaly when trying to use this tool. Until I selected some text in the editing window, the menu options for this tool were grayed out. However, after I selected some text, I was able to set up the options in the tool.

The settings for this tool are project specific. So, if you want to use the focus mode, you need to choose the focus options for each separate project.

There is a toolbar button to activate this tool. It is not part of the default options, so you'll need to customize your toolbar to add it.

Another helpful mode for some is the Scriptwriting Mode. I'll discuss this special writing mode next.

Scriptwriting Mode

I don't work in Scriptwriting Mode because I write fiction. I've never written a script. However, for those of you who do scriptwriting in Scrivener, it can be a valuable tool.

When you first open a project in Scrivener, in addition to fiction, nonfiction and academic options, there are several templates available for scriptwriting. These templates come pre-populated with options to make screenwriting easier. To enter Scriptwriting Mode press ⌘8 or Scriptwriting under the Format menu. When you do this, the Footer Status Bar changes to include new options. ⌘8 functions like a toggle switch. When you press ⌘8 again, you will return to the standard writing mode.

When you apply these options to your text, it formats it in the proper screenwriting format.

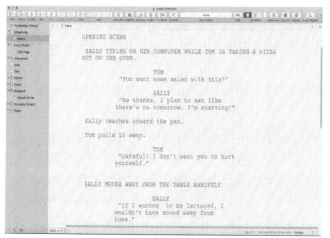

Figure 32: Sample of Screenwriting Mode

The Footer Status Bar will offer you several options for formatting different parts of your script.

Scene Heading	S
Action	A
Character	C
Parenthetical	P
Dialogue	D
Transition	T
Shot	H
✓ General Text	G
General Text (Centered)	E

Figure 33: Default Options in Scriptwriting Mode

Allowing Scrivener to automatically apply the proper formatting for each part of your script will speed up the process. If you press the function key together with the letter beside each element, the scriptwriting mode will type the text indicated by each letter.

When you're finished, the default output method and compile for scriptwriting mode is Front Page. However, you can output to other file types such as PDFs or Word documents.

Literature and Latte offers some helpful videos with examples and tips on using scriptwriting mode.

Now that we have explored many of the moving parts which make Scrivener a powerful piece of software, we're going to talk about how to customize it to work with your preferences. After all, these are your tools and they should suit your style of writing.

Chapter 3 – Making Scrivener Your Own

Scrivener is one of the most customizable programs I've ever used. There isn't much you can't change to accommodate your tastes. The philosophy behind Scrivener is that no one writes exactly the same as someone else. For example, I am a fan of customizing my toolbar and having everything at my disposal, while other writers much prefer using keyboard shortcuts. Still others prefer to navigate through menus. Scrivener allows you to do all of those things. You can customize the appearance of virtually everything in Scrivener.

Before Scrivener introduced their dark mode, I used to create different backgrounds for each project I was working on. I have worked on as many as four projects at once. It is nice to be able to tell them apart by just looking at the appearance of the project in front of me. To a certain extent, I still do this by changing the label colors of each character. (I typically write in first-person, alternating points of view, when I write fiction.) Changing the label colors allows me to know at a glance which project is open.

The default settings are easily changed and apply to all of your projects.

You can also set personal targets and deadlines and track your progress in Scrivener 3. There are new ways to visualize your progress without having to open other tools or windows.

You may have noticed that Scrivener 3 has a keyboard shortcut for nearly everything. In the section about keyboard shortcuts, I will provide a list of keyboard shortcuts to serve as a quick reference guide.

Toolbars are one of the most helpful features in Scrivener 3. We will discuss those next.

Customizing the Toolbar

A lot of features in Scrivener don't appear in other word processing programs. Therefore, the toolbar becomes an invaluable resource. You can display only icons or have the names of the tools appear below the icon. If you hover your mouse over each button, there is usually a helpful tooltip attached to help you navigate Scrivener 3 more efficiently.

To customize your toolbar, click on the View menu and then on Customize Toolbars.

If you are new to Scrivener, you may not know which options you will use most often on your toolbar. That's okay. You can add or subtract items from your toolbar when you get a better feel for which tools you use most often.

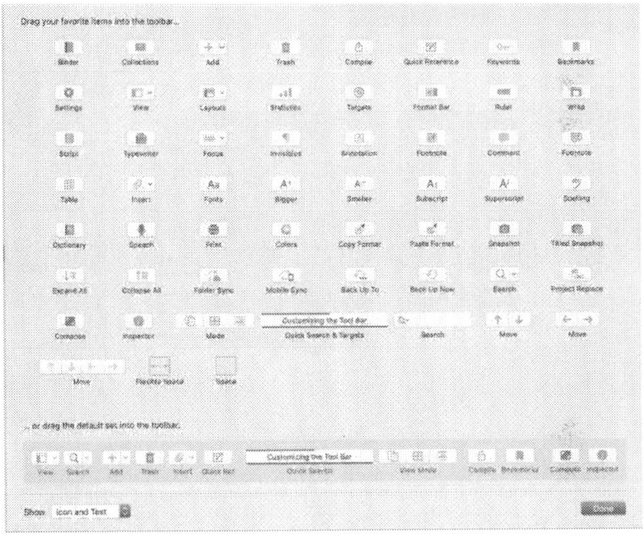

Figure 34: Options Under Customize Toolbar

Across the bottom of the bar you will see the default set of items in your toolbar. Below that, there is a menu which allows you to change the way the toolbar appears.

To add a tool to your toolbar, just click and drag it up to your existing toolbar. You can also adjust the spacing options, if you wish. Conversely, if you want to remove a tool from your toolbar, just open the Customize Toolbar tool and drag the icon you no longer wish to use from your toolbar back onto the icon options. A funny animation and sound effect will occur as your icon is obliterated. Never fear, if you want to put it back, it will be available from the icon menu.

There are some toolbar options I find indispensable. The move button, which helps you determine which level your document or folder is in in the Binder, is useful. I also add the expand and collapse tools because I use them frequently. Another helpful tool is the layout button. It allows you to instantly switch your layouts to include different things such as the outline or the corkboard. Additionally, it leads to another menu which allows you to analyze the frequency of word usage.

Scrivener has several types of redundancies built in. Often, there are three or four ways to accomplish nearly every task or feature Scrivener offers. The toolbar is only one mechanism for accessing these features. They are accessible via the menu or through keyboard shortcuts.

The toolbar is not the only area of Scrivener you can customize. You can also alter the appearance of the Scrivener interface to suit your needs.

Color your World ... or Not

I'll admit, I'm a very visual person. I love having the ability to customize my work environment to suit my project or even my mood. Fortunately, Scrivener 3 makes this process much easier. They have pre-existing things available in both light and dark mode. Although the pictures I've taken for this book are made using the light mode, when I don't have to document the steps I take and insert them into a book, I write in dark mode.

I am a chronic migraine sufferer. I started getting migraines in 2002. The ability to change the colors of the program in which I'm working has radically increased my ability to work in front of the computer without pain. Before the Mojave operating system and Scrivener introduced dark modes, I used to create them on my own by changing each element of Scrivener to a custom color. Thanks to the built-in settings in dark mode, I no longer have to do this.

How you choose for Scrivener 3 to appear on your screen doesn't have to have any bearing on the output of your manuscript. Feel free to write using colors you love. Later, I'll show you how to ensure the compile feature doesn't use any odd colors you write with.

I find it easier to customize my Scrivener interface if I modify an existing theme which is closest to how I want my projects to appear.

Clicking on the word Scrivener on the menu (beside the Apple symbol) will present to you a menu. Appearance is the second option. When you click on appearance, you will be given three options: System Default, light and dark. Choose your favorite.

The next option on this menu is Theme. There are pre-populated options available directly from Scrivener. Personally, I'm fond of A Midsummer Night. If the options available don't suit your fancy, check out the bulletin boards on Literature and Latte. They have several themes uploaded by users. You may have to unzip the file before you can import your new theme and, as always, when you download something from an unknown source, make sure you run a virus check. It's very easy to import a theme. When you do, it will appear on the menu of themes.

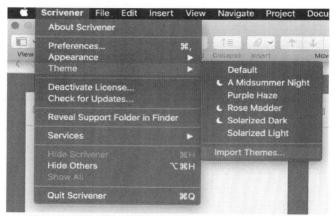

Figure 35: Importing Themes in Scrivener 3

If you want to develop your own theme, start with one that's closest to how you want your final theme to appear then go to Preferences (⌘,)

Click on the appearance tab and a menu of choices will appear.

The options which allow you to customize colors or fonts will show on those menus. Go through the sections you want to change and make the changes. A color selection tool will appear. Click on the color you want. The nice thing about this feature is that the changes appear in real time so you can check to see if you like the color.

Once you have changed all the options you wish, click on the Manage button and save your theme. Additionally, you can save the changes to a particular file if you don't want what you created to be applied globally.

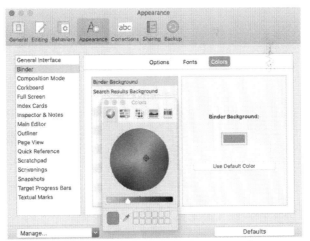

Figure 36: Changing Colors Under Preferences in Scrivener 3

As with all other types of customization and personal settings, I recommend that you export these items and save them on a thumb drive or an external backup drive. If something catastrophic happens to your computer or the Scrivener program, having these settings saved separately will help you restore your writing environment.

Figure 37: Saving Customized Preferences and Themes in Scrivener 3

Creating themes with your preferences for color and font is only one method for customizing your experience on Scrivener 3. Another key area involves setting the default behavior and settings for Document Mode (sometimes referred to as Scrivenings).

Changing and Setting Defaults

Scrivener's behavior and appearance depends a lot on its default settings for the Document Mode. Of course, in several places Scrivener gives you the opportunity to override your default settings with an alternative font. Still, it's helpful to set up your default editor in the style you prefer. If you choose N/A as your style layout in compile, whatever is in your default editor will appear. Basically, this is an as-is setting.

To change the default settings, go to Preferences (located under the word Scrivener) or press ⌘, to access the menu. From there, you will see the Edit tab. The first option is the Options menu. This allows you to set a few key settings including your default zoom, where the typewriter scroll feature appears, and how copy and paste information is treated.

My eyesight has never been spectacular. So, I appreciate the ability to set my default zoom at 250%. Additionally, I like to have my typewriter scroll appear in the middle of the compose window. Sadly, the typewriter tool only works in compose mode. I hope that in future upgrades, Scrivener will introduce this feature across other modes.

The next menu is formatting. This allows you to determine how new documents will appear in Scrivener.

You can set these preferences manually by making changes in the edit window under preferences. You can do things like set margins, default fonts, colors and spacing – like you would in any word processing program. If you are a fan of Microsoft Word, the default setting is similar to the normal template in Word.

You can also set the format of your footnotes in this section.

Although you can set up settings for things like margins, line spacing, fonts and indents manually, if you have another document in Scrivener where the settings are to your liking, you can open that document and set your preferences while in that document. Choose Edit, and then Formatting. Once you are on that window, choose Use Formatting in Current Editor. This button will make the formatting in your document apply to all new documents.

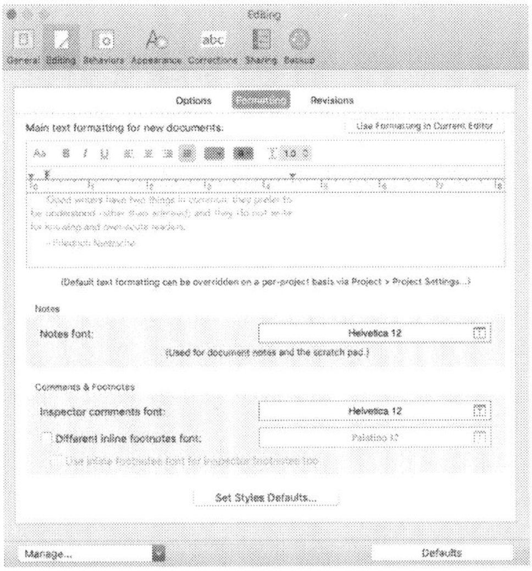

Figure 38: Setting Default Formatting Options under Preferences in Scrivener 3

If you have made substantial changes in this window, it is a good idea to save your preferences in a file separate from your computer's hard drive.

The last tab under editing menu is revisions. This allows you to apply custom colors to revision options. It is a common misconception that Scrivener has no way to track your changes when you are revising a document. You can show which text you add or subtract by choosing a revision color.

Revision Mode is located under the Format menu. When you go into Revision Mode, any changes you make will be in the revision color you choose. The Preferences menu allows you to change these colors to suit your needs. However, be aware that:

Unlike track changes in Microsoft Word, Scrivener doesn't make changes for you. In the revision mode, it just keeps track of the changes you have made.

After you have your writing environment customized to your taste, and you have set up the default settings for the editor, it is helpful to have a way to measure your progress on your manuscript. Scrivener 3 allows for different types of targets. I will discuss setting up targets to measure your progress in the next section.

Targets, Deadlines and Progress

As I have mentioned before, I am a sprinter. I like to keep track of how many words I write in a session. Fortunately, Scrivener makes this task easy.

The new quick search tool in Scrivener 3 makes it possible to see a visual representation of your progress toward your targets at a single glance.

It is great positive reinforcement to see the line indicating progress continue to grow and change colors throughout the process. As you can see in the figure below, it is still early in my writing day and I have written only one hundred and nineteen words this morning. I am approximately one-third finished with the word target I project for this book.

The top line represents my overall progress. The bottom line represents how much progress toward my goals I've made today. As you get closer to meeting your targets, the color will change. To meet my deadline, I need to write 1,131 words today. Of course, I'm crazy competitive with myself and I often try to beat the minimum number.

Figure 39: Progress Indicators in Quick Search box in Scrivener 3

To make this feature work properly, you need to set up the targets in your project. I have the target icon in my toolbar, but you can also get there by pressing ⇧⌘T or clicking on Project and then Show Project Targets.

By clicking on the options button, you can choose which documents to include in your count and set your deadline. If you click on session targets, you can choose the time at which you want the counts to reset and whether you will allow negative counts. Negative counts occur when you go back and edit your work and delete words. Unless I am shooting for a very specific word count, I often turn this feature off once I hit the editing stage. Sometimes, I just don't want to know how many of my words I've deleted.

You can also set targets for each individual document, folder, sub-document or sub-folder. You can have your progress displayed in Outline Mode and down at the bottom of your screen in the footer status bar.

To set a target for an individual document or folder, click on the target and a menu will appear which allows you to set your target as well as a minimum target and a maximum overrun.

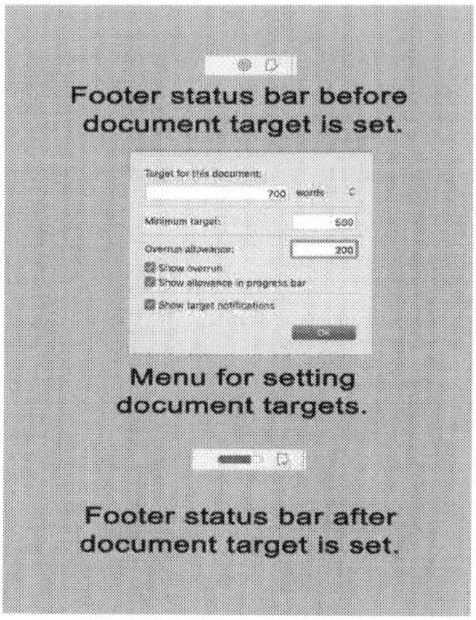

Figure 40: Setting Document Targets in Scrivener 3

I don't know if this will show up in the print or Kindle version, but if you'll notice on the green line there is a smaller vertical black line. This line indicates you have set a minimum target for this folder or document.

If you set a target before you duplicate your folder or document, the target will be duplicated as well.

If you have a project you use as a template, those targets will be saved from project to project.

If you are interested in sprints (a method of timed writing which greatly increases your productivity), I have put some links to sprinting resources in the resource guide.

Scrivener 3 has another tool, writing history, to track your progress. It is located under Project. It allows you to track your progress on your manuscript day by day.

Project targets are a great way to motivate yourself and keep track of your progress. Scrivener has many ways to help make your work more efficient. Keyboard shortcuts are one of those tools. We'll be discussing those next.

Keyboard Shortcuts

The great thing about Scrivener is it doesn't pin you down to one way to accomplish something. For example, if you want to add a new folder to your Binder, there are about five ways to accomplish this. You can click on the big green + in the toolbar, or, you can click on the folder with the + in the footer status bar, or you can add it under Project in the menu or, you can right-click on an existing folder in your Binder and click on add. The keyboard shortcut ⌥⌘N will also create a new folder.

This is only one example. The same holds true for many of the key functions in Scrivener. Fortunately, many of the keyboard shortcuts are listed in the menu.

For your convenience, I have provided an alphabetical chart of several of the keyboard shortcuts available in Scrivener 3.

 Be aware that if another program which is simultaneously running with Scrivener is using the same keyboard shortcuts for one of their functions, you may have difficulty using the keyboard shortcut assigned to Scrivener.

One example of this conflict is Mac's speech tool for reading back your text. This tool uses the same keyboard shortcut as Complete. (⌥ ESC). Therefore, when you try to use that keyboard shortcut, it performs the speech command instead.

CHART KEY:
- **⌘ = Command Key (Apple Key)**
- **^ = Control Key**
- **⌦ = Delete Key**
- **↓ = Down Arrow Key**
- **⏎ = Return Key**
- **← = Left Arrow Key**

- ⌥ = Option Key (Alt Key)
- → = Right Arrow Key
- = Shift Key
- ⇥ = Tab Key
- ↑ = Up Arrow Key

SCRIVENER
- Hide Others ⌥⌘H
- Hide Scrivener ⌘H
- Preferences ⌘,
- Quit and Close Windows ⌥⌘Q
- Quit Scrivener ⌘Q

FILE
- Close All ⌥⌘W
- Close Project and Clear Interface Settings ⌥⇧⌘W
- Close Project ⇧⌘W
- Close Window ⌘W
- Compile Draft... ⌥⌘E
- Export > Files... ⇧⌘E
- Import > Files... ⇧⌘I
- New Project ⇧⌘N
- Open... ⌘O
- Page Setup... ⇧⌘P
- Print Current Document... ⌘P
- Save and Rebuild Search Indexes ⌥⌘S
- Save As... ⇧⌘S
- Save ⌘S

EDIT
- Completions>Complete Document Title ^ESC

- Completions>Complete ⌥ESC
- Copy ⌘C
- Copy> Copy Special > Copy without Comments and Footnotes ⌥⇧⌘C
- Cut ⌘X
- Find > Find by Formatting ^⌥⌘F
- Find > Find Next Formatting ⌥⇧⌘G
- Find > Find Next ⌘G
- Find > Find Previous Formatting ^⌥⌘G
- Find > Find Previous ⇧⌘G
- Find > Find... ⌘F
- Find > Jump to Selection ⌘J
- Find > Quick Search ^⌥G
- Find> Use Selection For Find ⌘E
- Insert> Break> Line Break ⌥⌘
- Insert > Current Date & Time ⌥⇧⌘D
- Insert > Inline Footnote ^⌥F
- Link to Document > New Link... ⌘L
- Paste and Match Style ⌥⇧⌘V
- Paste ⌘V
- Project > Show Project Bookmarks ⌥⇧⌘B
- Redo ⇧⌘Z
- Select All ⌘A
- Select> Select Current Text ⌥⌘A
- Spelling and Grammar > Check Document Now ⌘;
- Spelling and Grammar > Check Spelling While Typing ⌘\
- Spelling and Grammar > Show Spelling and Grammar ⌘:
- Start Dictation ⌘⌘

- Undo ⌘Z

VIEW

- Corkboard> Show Status Stamps ^⌘S
- Corkboard Options > Show Keyword Colors ^⌘K
- Corkboard Options> Show Label Colors Along Edges ^⌘P
- Corkboard ⌘2
- Editor Layout > No Split ⌘'
- Editor Layout > Split Horizontally ⌥⌘=
- Editor Layout > Split Vertically ⌘"
- Enter Full Screen ^⌘F
- Enter/Exit Composition Mode ⌥⌘F (You can also use ESC to exit composition mode if this option is selected in Scrivener > Preferences: Compose.)
- Navigate >Next view (Next Pane) ^→ (This menu item cycles left to right through Binder, Left/Top Editor, Right/Bottom Editor, changing to the next target).
- Outline > Collapse All to Current Level ^⌘0
- Outline > Collapse All ⌘0
- Outline > Expand All ⌘9
- Outline ⌘3
- Project> Show Project Keywords ⇧⌘K
- Show/Hide Binder ⌥⌘B
- Show/Hide Inspector ⌥⌘I
- View > Text Editing > Show Page View ⌥⇧⌘P
- View> Scrivenings ⌘1
- Zoom > Zoom In ⇧⌘>
- Zoom > Zoom Out ⇧⌘<

PROJECT

- New Folder ⌥⌘N
- New From Template > First Template Document ⌥⇧⌘N (If you set a Template Folder, this shortcut is applied to the top document in the folder.)
- New Text ⌘N
- Project Settings... ⌥⌘,
- Project Statistics ⌥⇧⌘S
- Project Targets ⇧⌘T
- Show Project Bookmarks ⇧⌘B

DOCUMENTS

- Autofill> Set Selection as Title ⌥⇧⌘T
- Duplicate > with sub- documents and Unique Title ⌘D
- Duplicate > without sub- documents ⇧⌘D
- Duplicate> Set Synopsis from Main Text ⌥⇧⌘I
- Edit> Move> Move Left ^⌘←
- Edit> Move> Move Right ^⌘→
- Edit> Move> Move Down ^⌘↓
- Edit> Move> Move Up ^⌘↑
- Edit > Writing Tools > Linguistic Focus ^⌘L
- Group ⌥⌘G
- Merge ⇧⌘M
- Move to Trash ⌘⌫
- Navigate > Open > in (Left/Bottom) Editor ⌥⌘O
- Navigate > Open > in External Editor ^⌘O
- Navigate > Open > in Right/Top/Other Editor ⇧⌘O
- Navigate > Open > With all sub- documents >

On Editor Corkboard ⌥⇧⌘O

- Snapshot > Show Changes > Next Change ^⌘]
- Snapshot > Show Changes > Previous Change ^⌘[
- Snapshot > Take Snapshot With Title ⇧⌘5
- Snapshot > Take Snapshot ⌘5
- Split > at Selection ⌘K
- Split > with Selection as Title ⌥⌘K
- Ungroup ⌥⌘U

FORMAT

- Edit > Copy Formatting ^⌥⌘C
- Edit > Find> Search in Project ⇧⌘F
- Edit > Paste Formatting ^⌥⌘P
- Font > Bold ⌘B
- Font > Copy Font ⌥⌘C
- Font > Italic ⌘I
- Font > Paste Font ⌥⌘V
- Font > Show Colors ⇧⌘C
- Font > Show Fonts ⌘T
- Font > Underline > Single ⌘U
- Highlight > Highlight ⇧⌘H
- Insert> Bibliography/Citations... ⌘Y
- Insert > Comment ⇧⌘*
- Insert > Footnote ^⌘8
- Insert > Inline Annotation ⇧⌘A
- Paragraph > Center ⌘|
- Paragraph > Copy Paragraph Attributes ^⌘C
- Paragraph > Paste Paragraph Attributes ^⌘V
- Paragraph Justify ⌥⌘|
- Paragraph> Align Left ⌘{

- Paragraph> Align Right ⌘}
- Paragraph> Increase/Decrease Indents> Decrease Indents ⌥⌘←
- Paragraph> Increase/Decrease Indents> Increase Indents ⌥⌘→
- Paragraph>Increase/Decrease Indents> Decrease First Line Indents ^⌥⌘←
- Scriptwriting> Script Mode > Screenplay ⌘8
- Style> Block Quote ⌥⌘2
- Style> Caption ⌥⌘3
- Style> Centered Text ⌥⌘1
- Style> Heading 1 ⌥⌘4
- Style> Heading 2 ⌥⌘5
- Style> No Style ⌥⌘0
- Style> Show Styles Panel ^S
- View > Text Editing> Show/Hide Format Bar ⇧⌘R
- View > Text Editing> Typewriter Scrolling ^⌘T
- View> Text Editing> Show Ruler ⌘

NAVIGATE
- Binder ^⌥⌘B
- Editor > Backward in Document History ⌘[
- Editor > Forward in Document History ⌘]
- Editor > Lock in Place ⌥⌘L
- Go To > Enclosing Group ^⌘R
- Go To > Next Document ⌥⌘↓
- Go To > Previous Document ⌥⌘↑
- Go To>Next Document ⌥⌘↓
- Header Bar Title ^⌥⌘T
- Inspect > Comments and Footnotes ^⌥⌘K
- Keywords ^⌥⌘L

- Custom Metadata ^⌥⌘J
- Left Editor ^⌥⌘E
- Media > Fast Forward ⌥⌘}
- Metadata ^⌥⌘M
- Navigate> Go To > Selection ⌘4
- Notes ^⌥⌘H
- References ^⌥⌘N
- Reveal in Binder ⌥⌘R
- Right Editor ^⌥⌘R
- Scroll Down ^⌥⌘↓
- Scroll Up ^⌥⌘↑
- Snapshot ^⌥⌘M
- Synopsis ^⌥⌘I

WINDOW
- Float QuickReference Panels ^⌥⌘Q
- Layouts > Manage Layouts ⇧⌘)
- Minimize All ⌥⌘M
- Minimize ⌘M
- Zoom All ^⌥⌘-
- Zoom to Fit Screen ^⌘=
- Zoom ^⌘-
- Zoom> Zoom Out ⌘<

MISCELLANEOUS
- Document/Project Notes ⌘6
- Document/Project References ⌘6
- Help ⇧⌘?
- Open/Close Scratch Pad ⇧⌘

The Scratch Pad hot key can be set in Scrivener > Preferences: General Inspector

Now that you know about the key components of Scrivener 3 and how they work together and you know how to customize the settings in Scrivener to work best with your writing style, it's time to talk about the best practices in Scrivener 3 for saving your valuable work.

Chapter 4 – Document Safety Protocol

Writing is tough work. It's even tougher when you have to redo it because of lost or corrupt files. Scrivener does everything in its power to make sure this doesn't happen to you. Even so, it is best to prepare for something catastrophic.

Unfortunately, I have first-hand knowledge of this. Several years ago, I had computer problems which I was unaware of. These problems caused my software to become unstable and not work as it was supposed to. Sadly, I lost about fifteen thousand words of my work-in-progress. It was completely devastating and demoralizing.

It was also a profound learning experience. Even if you think your backup protocol is solid, it is good to build in redundancy. So, this section is about setting up Scrivener to protect your work and building in redundancy to your file management to prevent loss. Fortunately, Scrivener 3 has several tools to help protect your project from data loss.

Setting up Automatic Backup Feature

The first tool in Scrivener 3's arsenal to protect you from data loss is the Automatic Backup Feature.

You can set up this feature from the Preferences menu (⌘,) by selecting the backup option.

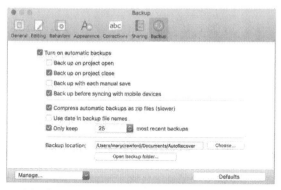

Figure 41: Setting up Automatic Backup Feature for Scrivener 3 in Preferences

If you have the hard drive space, I recommend keeping the greatest number of recent backups. Since I use the Time Machine feature to back up my files on my MacBook Pro, I could backup my files on my actual hard drive. However, if you don't backup your files externally on a regular basis, you might want to choose a location on the cloud. I have chosen to back up my projects upon closing them. However, you can choose different options if you wish.

Cloud services which may not play well with Scrivener 3 when working with live files work just fine for saving your backup files since they are zipped.

You can also manually backup your files. To do this, you can click on File ▸ Backup. Optionally, you can add an icon to your toolbar.

The Automatic Backup Feature is not the only protection you have for your files. Next, we'll discuss the role of Snapshot in protecting your data.

Snapshot

The Snapshot feature is just what it sounds like. It allows you to take a picture of a moment in time of your folders and documents. As a subtle reminder to myself to use this feature more often, I have placed it in my toolbar. However, if you have not done so, you can access this feature through the document menu. If you want to save a Snapshot with a title, the keyboard shortcut is ^⌘5. If you don't wish to include a title, the keyboard shortcut is ⌘5. Personally, I find it helpful to add a title so I know what I'm looking at later. I will often note the changes I have made in a particular Snapshot. It is a good idea to take a Snapshot every time you make substantial changes to your document.

Honestly, I don't use the Snapshot feature as often as I should. Because this feature differs from the software I grew up using, I forget the feature is there. However, it is very helpful when you are making edits because you can compare the differences in Snapshot. The Snapshot feature allows you to roll back your folder or document to a previous version if you don't like the changes you've made. If your file has a Snapshot attached to it, it will have a special indicator on the folder or document. The corner of the document in the folder will be folded down.

To work with your Snapshot, look for the camera icon in the Inspector. If you have a Snapshot in a folder, a little dot will appear above the camera in the Inspector. The date and title of your Snapshot will appear in the menu. You can compare Snapshot or rollback your document to a previous version.

By using the Snapshot manager, you can compare Snapshot by phrase or paragraph and export your Snapshot to another kind of file. Documents ▸ Snapshot ▸ Snapshot Manager. To export your Snapshot, click on the gear in the bottom left-hand corner.

If you are syncing with the iOS version, turn on the feature which will take a Snapshot when you update your file. To do this, click on preferences and then sharing. Under the sync tab, there are several options for syncing your files - including one to take Snapshot.

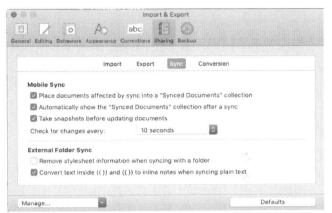

Figure 42: Settings to Automatically Take Snapshot when Syncing Your Files.

In addition to working with the Automatic Backup feature and Snapshot, you can also save your files to your Dropbox. In the next section, I will discuss Dropbox and other cloud services.

Saving to the Cloud

For your own peace of mind, you may use a cloud service to save your Scrivener files. This option is helpful if you are using Scrivener on several computers. If you are using the iOS version of Scrivener together with the Mac version, you'll need Dropbox to sync your files.

If you don't backup your hard drive to an external device, you might consider saving your backup copies of Scrivener files to a cloud service.

Regardless of which cloud service you choose, make sure you wait until your file is fully saved before you close Scrivener. Failing to do so can cause corruption in your file. If you're using Dropbox, you can watch the progress of your save on the Dropbox icon in your Mac toolbar.

Dropbox

If you use a cloud service to save your files as you work with them, Literature and Latte recommends Dropbox. Dropbox has recently updated its paid service to include a rollback feature if something catastrophic has occurred to your current file. This works a lot like the Time Machine on the Mac platform.

 If you use Dropbox, it is critically important that you allow the project to completely finish saving before you close Scrivener.

The iOS version of Scrivener works well with Dropbox and makes switching back and forth between the Mac version and iOS easy. Just make sure you save the file in an area the iOS program can locate.

Please enter a name for this theme:

Mary's custom light theme

Themes save only the main appearance preferences, such
as colors and corkboard settings.

Settings to include in theme

- ☑ Main color & theme settings
- ☑ Composition mode theme settings
- ☑ Binder font settings
- ☑ Outliner font settings
- ☑ Corkboard font settings
- ☑ Header bar font
- ☑ Scrivenings title settings
- ☑ Scrivenings separator settings

The theme will be saved in Scrivener's Application Support
folder and will be available in the "Manage..." and
"Scrivener" menus.

Cancel   OK

Figure 43: Saving Themes to File in Scrivener 3

There are other things which need to be exported and saved as well. You can save Section Types by right clicking on a file in your Binder and clicking on Section Types and going down to the bottom of the menu and clicking on edit. After you've done that, click on Section Types and export.

Unfortunately, status and label features don't have the same import and export ability. However, you can highlight the status or label types you want to use in another project and drag them over to the new project.

Under compile, you can export your formats in either Scrivener 3 or Scrivener 2 formats if you need a backward compatibility.

This is helpful if you want to work on Scrivener 3 projects in Windows. As of the end of October 2019, Scrivener 3 for Windows has not yet been released and in order to have compatibility between file types, you must work with your project in Scrivener 3 for Mac as a Scrivener 2 project. There is good news coming. Based on the beta version of Scrivener 3 for Windows, it appears Literature and Latte has built in direct compatibility into the next version.

Now that you've learned how to back up your project and settings, I'd like to talk about some best practices for ensuring your work against catastrophe I've discovered the hard way.

Best Practices

As I mentioned before, nothing teaches you the really hard lessons like an epic computer failure. After I lost fifteen thousand words, I became much more diligent about my redundancy and file management. I know some of this might seem extreme, but peace of mind is worth a lot.

After I had my catastrophic data loss, I discovered the Time Machine feature built into Mac OS. It has become one of my favorite features on my MacBook Pro. For those of you who are not familiar with this feature, your Time Machine on a Mac is an easy way to back up to an external drive. The Time Machine works in the background and is unobtrusive. It allows you to save your entire hard drive and your applications. If you have to restore your information to another Mac computer, it is simple to do. It is also simple to restore files which have been corrupted. You simply choose a date in which your file was operating properly and click restore.

In addition to the Time Machine, I save all of my Scrivener files in my Dropbox account. To me, it is worth the nominal fee to back my files up on the cloud. Of all the cloud services which allow you to save live files of your work-in-progress, Dropbox is the most compatible with Scrivener.

If you wish, you can also use programs like Carbonite to give yourself another layer of protection.

Because I don't want to deal with the consequences of major data loss again, I take some additional steps. Whether you will be as fastidious about backing up your Scrivener projects or not is up to you.

Every few months, I save all of my Scrivener files onto a thumb drive in addition to using Time Machine and Dropbox.

I can't repeat this often enough.

 When you are saving your files, make sure your computer is done with the process before you close Scrivener. If you don't do this, it can corrupt your files.

I have gotten into the habit of compiling my Scrivener project every day or so and sending myself a copy of my Word document via Facebook. If you don't want to use Facebook, you can also just email yourself a copy. Although restoring from a Word document would take some time, having a Word document is better than having no copy of your work-in-progress. I have spoken to several authors who have had their laptops stolen or destroyed and as a result, they lost all of their writing. It is a heartbreaking scenario to consider. It might be worth the extra step in case the worst happens.

Now that we have discussed the parts of Scrivener, their function and how to safely protect your words, let's talk about working with your manuscript in Scrivener.

Chapter 5 – Working with a Manuscript

When I started working with Scrivener, I was in the middle of a project. It was no problem because Scrivener 3 is flexible. Not only can you start a project from scratch in Scrivener, you can also easily import an existing manuscript written in another application. So, I will talk about ways to start a manuscript, import a manuscript and apply different formatting tools like styles, labels, Section Types and special formatting.

Starting from Scratch

I have touched on this briefly, but you can easily start a document from scratch in Scrivener 3. If the project template window does not open for you, press ⇧ ⌘N or choose new project under the file menu.

You will be presented with a variety of templates available by default from Scrivener or any templates you have imported.

To start a new project, simply choose the template that's closest to what you would like to accomplish. However, if you want the features from another type of template, you can add those files to your project by creating a project with the alternative template and dragging the folders over to your Binder in your work in process. Don't worry about picking exactly the right template. The contents of your Binder can always be adjusted and expanded. For example, if you choose a short story template and your work-in-progress ends up being a novel, you can always add more folders to your Binder.

You will be asked to save your project immediately. If you later change your mind and want to call your project something else, it is easiest to change it in the Finder program on your Mac computer. Just use the re-name feature.

Scrivener 3 has added a handy feature to the file menu called Favorite Projects. If the project you have created is one you plan to access frequently, you may want to add your project to this list. Unlike recent documents, this list stays constant regardless of how many other files you have opened. To add a file to this list, choose File > Add Project to Favorites. This feature will sort your projects alphabetically to make them easier to find when you have several.

Once you have created your project, you will have a Binder on the left-hand side of the page. You can write directly into Scrivener by choosing the Scrivenings mode. Most of your manuscript needs to go in the Draft Folder. Your front and back matter are the exception to this rule. They go in the Research Folder. As mentioned before, the other two mandatory folders are research and the Trash Folder. If you have extraneous material such as pictures, charts, audio clips, video clips or Excel files, they can all go in the Research Folder.

You can add additional folders and scenes to the Draft Folder.

Alternatively, if you like to plan your work before you start to write, you can use the corkboard or outline view.

Personally, I prefer to set up my page parameters in page set up under the file menu. (⇧⌘P) Although I do finish formatting using Microsoft Word when I am finished with my manuscript, choosing the page size and margins gives me a rough idea of how my project flows on the page when I use the page view settings. To access the page view, go to View ▸ Text Editing and click on Show Page View.

You may be thinking to yourself that's fine if I'm starting from scratch. However, I already have a manuscript started in another program like Microsoft Word. That's okay, Scrivener has a mechanism for importing files from other applications. We will discuss that next.

Importing Work Done in Other Applications

Scrivener has two ways to import documents created in other applications. The first is a straight import function. I rarely use this type of import because I prefer Scrivener's more effective alternative, Import and Split. Import and Split allows you to mark up a copy of your original document and then import it into chapters.

First, I'll talk about the simple import procedure, then I will move on to Import and Split.

Import

Scrivener 3 can import your files from Microsoft Word, OpenOffice. These files can be stored in your Draft Folder – just make sure your Draft Folder (or a sub-folder you've created) is clicked in your Binder before you import. Make sure you know where your document is located. I don't typically use this feature much because I have written in Scrivener for nearly five years. So, when I was experimenting with this option, I inadvertently tried to import a very large file with over three thousand documents in it. Fortunately, I was able to cancel the transfer before much damage was done. Even if the files had been transferred to my Binder or Research Folder, I could easily move them to the trash.

If you import images or websites into your Binder, you need to place them in your Research Folder. However, if you need to use images in your project, there is a different procedure to accomplish that. I will discuss using images in your project in Chapter 9.

At the moment, Scrivener 3 uses Java to import your files. However, they are testing a new conversion tool. If you wish, Literature & Latte provides instructions on how to change your preferences to use their new conversion tool. You can find more information about this at https://www.literatureandlatte.com/forum/viewto pic.php?t=56863.

If your document is in PDF form or was created in Pages, you will need to convert it to a Word or RTF document first. The same is true for .EPUB and .MOBI files.

Although it is relatively painless to import files into Scrivener, sometimes a file may arrive as one big block of text. Fortunately, Scrivener has an answer to this problem. The solution is called Import and Split.

Import and Split

The Import and Split feature was one of the first tools I ever used in Scrivener. I suspect that might be true for many of you too. This tool is very useful if you have created a document in another application which you need broken down into the proper folders in your Binder.

To use the Import and Split function, I recommend you create a working copy of your Microsoft Word document (just for safekeeping).

The next step in the process involves giving Scrivener some cues about where you would like the splits to occur in your pre-existing document. Personally, I like to use $&$ as my markers because that combination of characters is not likely to appear in my document naturally.

Open the working document you created. Every place you want to separate into a folder such as your dedication, copyright or forward as well as every chapter (and scene, if you wish), you need to place the symbols to alert Scrivener 3 of your intent.

You can do this function with a global search and replace. Which symbol you use depends upon how you've constructed your Microsoft Word document. Some people use page breaks. In search and replace, this symbol is ^m. Other authors prefer to use section breaks. In Microsoft Word, this is represented by ^b. If you use section breaks instead of page breaks, you must do one more step of preparation. To make the process smoother (because of Microsoft Word's limitations on Find and Replace), you should do a global find and replace to substitute page breaks for section breaks. To prepare your document for Import and Split if you have used section breaks, you would type the following:

Find: ^b
Replace with: ^m

After you have page breaks, then do the following search and replace function:

Find: ^m
Replace with: $&$ ^m

This function places $&$ at the end of each section of your document. This will enable Scrivener 3 to split your document into individual folders when you import.

To start the process of Import and Split, go to file ▸ Import ▸ Import and Split. Then choose the working file you created.

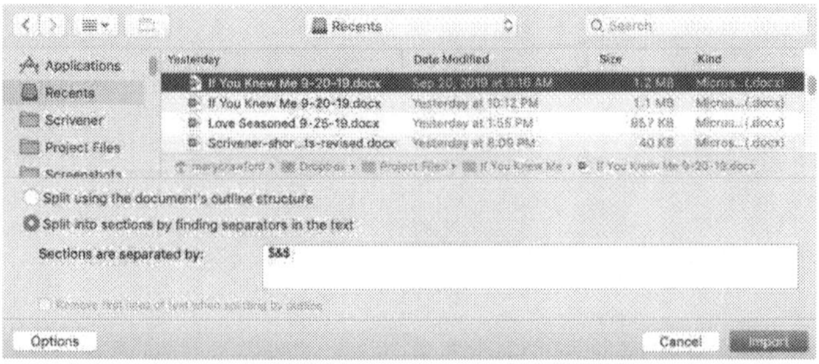

Figure 44: Import and Split Menu in Scrivener 3

You'll note that the special symbols we placed in our working document are in the window which determines how the sections are separated. You can change the symbols to anything you wish. Just make sure they are consistent between your working document and the Import and Split window.

If you used the outline feature in Microsoft Word to create your manuscript, you can split your document according to its outline structure.

Then, click on import. It is important to pay attention to what is selected in your Binder before you click import. The first few times I tried to use this tool, I was not cognizant of this factor. Sometimes, my imported document landed in the Trash Folder. If that happens to you, you can just drag it up to your Draft Folder.

Magic will happen – yes, I know it's actually computer programming – but it seems like magic when your document appears in the Binder presorted into documents. If you prefer to work in folders rather than documents, you can highlight the documents in your Binder and right-click on them. This will give you an option to convert your documents to folders.

Figure 45: Documents Created by Import and Split

Doing a global search and replace works really well if your original document has labels on each section. Sometimes you may work with a document with no such titles. In that case, Scrivener will display the first eight or nine words in each section as the title of the document.

If your working document does not have titles before each section, you can either change the name of each imported document in your Binder or you can add a title below each separator in your working document before you perform the import. This is my preferred method if I'm trying to assign chapters to a block of text.

If you want to select multiple folders in your Binder, you can press the ⇧ to choose the first and last folder and everything in between will be selected. Or, if you want to choose each folder individually, you can use the ⌘ to choose multiple folders.

Sometimes we authors change our mind about where scenes should go or how they are arranged. That's okay, Scrivener has you covered with the Split and Merge functions. You can adjust your document on the fly without having to copy and paste. We will talk about this handy tool next.

Split and Merge

One of the handiest features in Scrivener 3 is its ability to split and merge documents without having to copy and paste. I use this feature most often when I am editing and I realize that I need to add a section break because the action takes place in a different time frame or location.

Before I discovered Scrivener, I used to manually divide my scenes through copy and paste. Now, if I want to split a scene into two, I can place my cursor before the first word of the part I want in a different folder and click on Document ‣ Split.

Scrivener 3 will add the second portion of your document to a new file. So, if your scene was called Scene 2, the new file will be Scene 2-1. The synopsis, notes and comments will remain with the first file. If you need them in both, you must copy and paste the information into your new file.

When using the split feature, you can place words at the beginning of the area you want to split off and select them. These words will become the title of your new folder.

Let's say you got a little too ambitious with your scene dividing or you simply decide the smaller scenes work better as one larger scene. No problem. It's an easy fix with Scrivener 3.

Highlight the folders you want to merge in your Binder. Then click on Document ‣ Merge or use ⇧⌘M on your keyboard. Your files or documents will be combined into the top file or document you clicked. The Metadata from the documents will be combined.

Sometimes, you may need to export a file from Scrivener. We'll talk about that next.

Export

I don't use the export feature of Scrivener often. However, it is useful for a couple of things. First, if you are working with Scrivener across platforms, Scrivener 3 projects are not yet compatible with the Scrivener for Windows. Therefore, to work on your project in Windows, you need to export it as a Scrivener 2 project. Out of an abundance of caution, I recommend that you indicate that it is a Scrivener 2 project somewhere in the title. If I am working with the Windows platform, I will use the title of the project and add for Windows on the end. It can get confusing to work with multiple versions of the same file (regardless of which software you use) therefore, I try to make it crystal clear if I have created an alternative version of my main file. I use Scrivener files as master files. So, it is important for me to keep them straight so I know that I'm always working on the most recent version. Don't ask me how I reached this conclusion. It's a very sad, ugly story.

To export and convert a Scrivener 3 file to Scrivener 2, click on File ▸ Export ▸ As Scrivener 2 project. After you've done this, you can either work with your Scrivener 2 project in the old version of Scrivener 2 for Mac or in Scrivener 1 for Windows.

The iOS version of Scrivener will work with either Scrivener 3 or Scrivener 2 projects. So, if you are working with all three platforms, you will need your project to be in Scrivener 2 format.

The other cool thing you can export are your comments and in-line annotations. Many authors like to use the comment feature to keep running notes to themselves or to assist with editing. In-line annotations can work the same way. In fact, you can color code them to show point of view, progression along a timeline or virtually anything else. You can even drag a picture of your character into the comments or annotations if you need a quick reference. Scrivener makes it possible for you to export all these comments and annotations.

To export your annotations, click on File ▸ Export ▸ Comments and Annotations. A menu will appear and you can limit the export to just the current selected file (among other things).

Sync

The sync function is another option I don't use often. I prefer to use compile instead for most functions. However, there are a couple of situations in which the sync function might be helpful. To reach the sync menu, click on File ▸ Sync.

First, there is an option to sync to mobile devices. Selecting this option will force Scrivener to check against your mobile devices to determine whether your project needs to be updated. According to Literature and Latte, you should not have to use this feature to work with the iOS version of Scrivener. However, if you are uncertain whether your file has properly synced, it isn't harmful to use this function.

Additionally, you can sync text or RTF files to external folders. This might be a helpful feature if you are working in collaboration with someone else. For example, you can import the text files into Google docs. If you are a screenwriter, there is an option to export the files in a format compatible with Final Draft. You can elect to Sync your entire Draft Folder or individual parts.

 Do not use the sync with External Folder function to update your files in the IOS version of Scrivener.

Now, I'll turn to changing the way your document appears on-screen Styles, a new feature in Scrivener 3.

Styles

Styles are new in Scrivener 3. However, if you have used earlier versions of Scrivener, you are likely familiar with the features included in Styles. Styles are just a name for a group of formatting characteristics which you can save for later use. Personally, I am a big fan of the Styles function because it allows me to have consistent formatting throughout my entire series.

The older versions of Scrivener had Formatting Presets, but that feature was not as robust as the new Styles feature.

Scrivener 3 allows you to assign fonts, colors, spacing and indents to a style. If you change a style in Scrivener 3, the changes are automatically applied to all the text which has been assigned to that particular title. This feature is helpful if you decide to change your formatting midway through a project.

Scrivener 3 comes with some Styles already defined. They are located on your format bar and include things like headings, title, attribution, and block quotes. If you choose No Style, your document is formatted according to the default settings under preferences.

If you choose block quote as a style, it won't be justified on both sides because of a limitation in Scrivener. It will, however, be indented.

If none of Scrivener 3's preset Styles meet your needs, you can add your own. There are several ways to accomplish this. You can adapt an existing style with your own font color or spacing choices. After you have made the appropriate changes to the text, simply highlight the text that is representative of what you want your Style to be and add it to the list of Styles. To do this, you can click on the Show Styles Panel which is at the end of the menu of your existing styles. Then just click the plus sign and a menu will appear which looks like this:

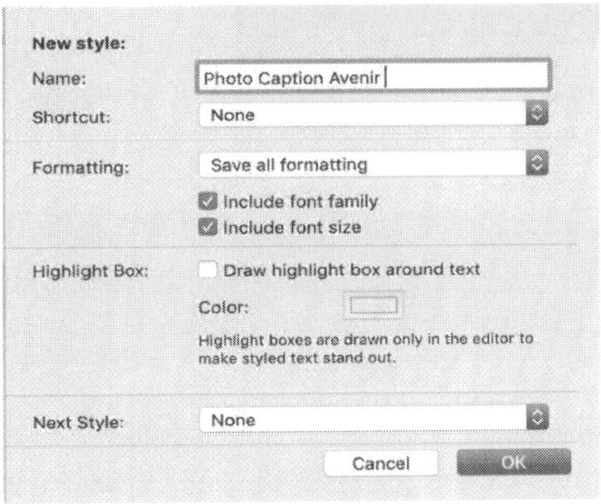

New style:

Name:	Photo Caption Avenir
Shortcut:	None
Formatting:	Save all formatting
	☑ Include font family
	☑ Include font size
Highlight Box:	☐ Draw highlight box around text
	Color:
	Highlight boxes are drawn only in the editor to make styled text stand out.
Next Style:	None

Cancel   OK

Figure 46: Adding a New Style to Scrivener 3

Most of the time when I add a new Style, I don't save all the formatting. I select Save Paragraph Style instead. I've learned the hard way that saving all the formatting can wipe out existing italics or bold formatting. Here, I want the style to include bold and italics, so I chose to save all the formatting. Personally, I don't use a lot of keyboard shortcuts because of my mobility limitations. However, you can assign keyboard shortcuts to individual styles. If you are working with a lot of different styles in a single document, you may have the styles highlighted in a particular color.

I feel the need to make a small confession here. I set up the style to make my photo captions in Scrivener 3. Later, I went back to add a highlight box around to my style so I could tell when I applied it. Unfortunately, when I did that, I inadvertently selected the picture too. Therefore, when I applied my style the next time, it replaced my graphic with the one I have included in the style. Fortunately, I discovered this right away or it could have resulted in a long reedit. So, after I discovered my mistake, I selected the proper portion of my caption and then went to Format ▸ Style ▸ Redefine Style from Selection. This brings up a menu for you to select your choices. This time, I chose save paragraph style and added a highlight box.

You can also assign a style type to existing text. This is my favorite way to create styles. I simply open a file which contains text that is formatted the way I prefer and then I go to Format ▸ Style ▸ New style from selection. This sequence brings up the same menu as above. You can keep all formatting, paragraph formatting or character formatting.

Remember we talked about indents on the ruler tool before? I use New Style From Selection to create a non-indented version of my existing styles. I use these styles after a section break or for the first paragraph of my chapter. To create this, I use a paragraph that's already formatted to my liking. If that paragraph is already indented, I drag the indent on the ruler so that the beginning of my text is lined up with the rest of the paragraph. Then, I save the non-indented paragraph as a style all of its own. For example, I have Garamond Indented and Garamond No Indent.

Ironically, there is no mechanism to export your styles. However, you can import them from one project to another. To do so, simply open the show styles panel at the bottom of your style list and click on the gear. After you've done that, import styles is at the bottom of the list. It will direct you to open a Scrivener file. Just choose the Scrivener file which has the styles you wish to transfer to your new project.

In addition to styles, you may work with labels in your project.

Labels

Labels are, not surprisingly, exactly what they sound like. They are a mechanism to add more information to your project. You can have the labels show up in your section formatting.

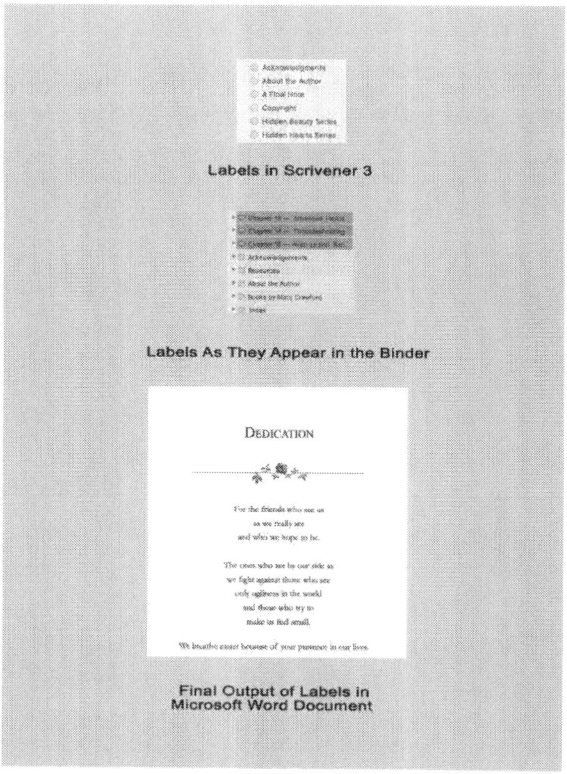

Figure 47: Labels in Scrivener 3

Although in some sections of my manuscript, I use the label function in my chapter headings, you don't have to. You can use labels to track all types of things from point of view, to the progress you've made in your manuscript. In fact, the way I use labels changes during the progress of writing a book.

Since I frequently work on more than one project at once, I change the label color for my characters so it is easy for me to tell at a glance which file I'm working on. Then, when I get to the editing process, I change the label colors to show what I need to work on. For example, if I need to add more detail about a couple's relationship, I change the color of the label to bright yellow to remind me to go back into that particular file and adjust the content. I do the same thing for location details or pacing issues. Using labels allows me to continue editing while marking potential issues with my manuscript. If your story takes place in different time periods, you can use labels to remind you to anchor your scenes on a timeline.

 If you change your labels during the editing process and you use them in your compile settings, make sure you change them back before you compile.

Labels are easy to use. To get started, you can add a label by clicking on the footer bar status under the Inspector. Alternatively, you can right-click on the document or file in your Binder to attach a label. If you want to edit the labels, scroll down to the individual list and click on edit. You can change both the text and the color.

If the labels don't appear in your Binder, there is an option under view to change the way labels appear. You can include them in your Binder, your outline or your index cards on your corkboard. In Scrivener 3, you can either display the label colors as a dot next to your text or you can have the label color show as a background color across your Binder.

Labels are a simple way to add information in context to your folders or documents in Scrivener. In the next section, I'll discuss a more complex feature new to Scrivener 3: Section Type.

Section Type

The introduction of the Section Types is one of the most visible changes in Scrivener 3. Personally, I think it's also one of the most helpful. In previous editions of Scrivener, it is difficult to visualize formatting changes as you apply them. The introduction of Section Types changes all that.

One concept that was foreign to me when I started using Scrivener was the idea that it didn't matter how I set up Scrivener during the writing process, compiling could change everything without impacting my manuscript in the Binder. Once you realize that these processes are largely separate, it is easier to understand the compile function.

The first step in using the new compile set up is to assign Section Types. This is not the same as assigning Styles to change the way your project appears on the screen. Assigning Section Types just categorizes different types of content in your Binder. For example, the following are Section Types I use when writing my romance novels.

Structure-Based

Back matter with Headers
Title Page
Chapter Heading
Scene
✓ Chapter
Epilogue
Heading
First Scene
Front Matter
Front Matter with Headers
N/A

Default Subdocument Type
✓ Structure-Based
Back matter with Headers
Title Page
Chapter Heading
Scene
Chapter
Epilogue
Heading
First Scene
Front Matter
Front Matter with Headers
N/A

Edit...

Figure 48: An Example of Customized Section Types in Scrivener 3

There are several ways to assign Section Types. First, as shown above, you can click on the Metadata tab in your Inspector and assign each file or document its own Section Type. Additionally, you can right-click on a folder or document in your Binder and assign it that way.

 You can highlight several folders or documents by pressing ⌘ while you click on folders or documents . You can then assign Section Types in bulk.

If you are a fan of outlining, you can have Section Type show in your outline and adjust your Section Types there.

Section Types can also be assigned in the compile window. When you check the box to include a folder in compile, just click on the down arrow to bring up your menu of Section Types. Another cool feature of the compile menu is its ability to show you which Section Types are applied to each document.

In the following example, I have selected first scene in the Section Layout window. The compiler automatically highlights all the files in my document which are assigned to the first scene Section Type.

I created a special first scene format because I format the first few words of each first section in small caps.

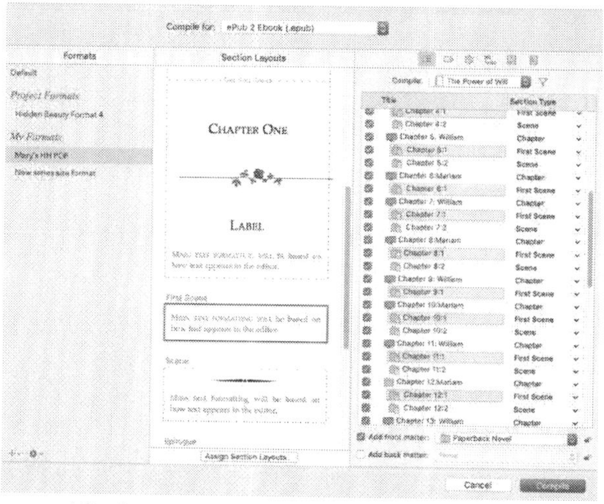

Figure 49: Section Layout Indicators in Scrivener 3

There is one more slightly complex way of assigning section layouts in bulk. To reach this window, click on project settings under project - or use the keyboard shortcut ⌥⌘, . Then, click on Section Types

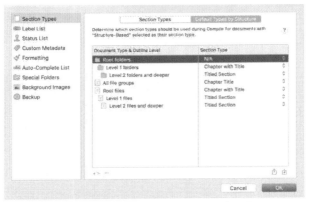

Figure 50: Adding Section Types by Structure

Clicking on default type by structure allows you to assign different Section Types based on the level your files appear in your Binder. For example, in the above illustration, every file that is in Level 2 or deeper, will be automatically assigned to the Titled Section section type.

 Note: if you have a template or a file you use as a template, you can assign Section Types to your template and they will be saved across projects created with those templates.

You may be thinking to yourself, "Okay, I've assigned section layouts, but now what?"

This is the part of the process that's difficult to put into words for people who have never used Scrivener before. I will try to describe the process in simple terms. When your document is in the Binder in Scrivener, it is somewhat analogous to a draft document. It's not a direct correlation because before Scrivener 3 arrived, I used to format my work in the Scrivenings pane exactly how I wanted it to appear in the final document and chose the as-is option when compiling. You can still do this, but working with section layouts is much more straightforward and if you use graphics as scene separators, you can save yourself on delivery service fees by automating the process with section layouts.

Anyway, if you envision the work in your Binder as a rough draft that still needs to go to the formatter or typesetter, it helps explain the role of the compiler and section layout.

When you open the compile menu, you will be presented with three panes. On the left-hand side is the format pane. Think of these as the options the printer or formatter offer. (You can customize these, and I will discuss formats under Demystifying the Compiler in Chapter 12.) The type of formats offered depends on the output you want. For example, they are different for an e-book than they are for a Word document.

In the middle section is a list of your section layouts. This section tells the formatter how you want each part of your document handled.

On the right-hand side is where you tell the formatter which parts of your manuscript you would like to be included in your final output.

To select all the files or documents at once, press the option key while you click in one of the check boxes.

If you have forgotten to select a Section Type for your document, you can add it from this window in compile.

Once you have selected the files from your Binder that you want to appear in your output and assign each folder or document, you can click option and compile. This will save the configuration for later use.

To compile the manuscript into a formatted document, first, you need to choose an output format. The compile feature has dozens of options. I usually use two of these options in my writing but your choices may be different. I either compile to an .EPUB or a Microsoft Word document. Although you can save your file as a .MOBI file, I don't bother any more. I just upload an .EPUB when I post my e-books to Amazon.

On the left-hand side of the compile window is the format pane. Scrivener has a list of default formats available. These options will change depending on your output. For example, if you are outputting to a text document, your formatting options are limited.

In our analogy, this formatting option is like choosing a style for your formatter or typesetter to follow. For example, for my fiction, I have created chapter headings with specific graphics for each series and I format the first few words of each first scene with small caps. These custom touches are determined by each format. If you need to adjust the default formats, you can right-click on a format and click duplicate and save. Formats can either be attached to each project or be saved as globally available within Scrivener.

The middle section of the Compile Window is where you assign your Section Types to the format you have chosen. This is like telling your formatter how to treat each element of your manuscript. In Scrivener 3, the first time you use a format for each type of output, you will need to assign your Section Types. After that, Scrivener 3 will remember your choices for the next time you compile.

I hope this overview of the role of Section Types in the new compile system helps clarify things. I will be discussing the compiler in more detail in Chapter 12.

Formatting

There are some random remarks I want to make about formatting.

First, under the Format menu, there is an option to format lists. This can be handy. However, remember your lists may look different when they are rendered on an e-book device because each reader has the opportunity to set their own font and spacing.

It is important to remember e-book and paperback formats need to be handled differently. Unlike paperbacks, e-book readers have the option to change the way fonts appear. E-book readers have a limited number of fonts available. If you have your heart set on a particular font for chapter headings or pullout quotes in your book and you want them to remain consistent in the e-book format, you'll need to save your font as a .JPEG or .PNG file.

Here is an example from an old version of one of my books. Incidentally, this is also the way I format my title pages which are a little on the fancy side.

CHAPTER 8

Figure 51: Chapter Heading Formatted in Photoshop

As pretty as these graphics are, there are some inherent downsides. First, including graphics like this increases your delivery cost (if you choose the 70% royalty option on Amazon).

Another consideration is accessibility. Many people rely on screen readers and graphics do not translate well. One way to minimize this downside is to supply alternative descriptions for your graphics.

There is an interesting feature of formatting within Scrivener. Your font choices and compile can be easily overridden. For example, if you are submitting your manuscript to an anthology and the curators of the anthology expect your document in Times New Roman and that is not typically what you use, you can override the styles to include Times New Roman.

This setting is located above the Section Layout Pane of the Compile window. There is a drop-down menu which says Font: If you assign a font here, it will override your Section Layout options.

I always have to search for this feature when I need it. So, I will highlight it here. If you need to change your text to superscript or subscript (as in the word 2nd) you can change the alignment under Format ▸ Font ▸ Baseline. It is important to note that when you are finished using alternative formatting, you need to go back to the menu and choose Use Default.

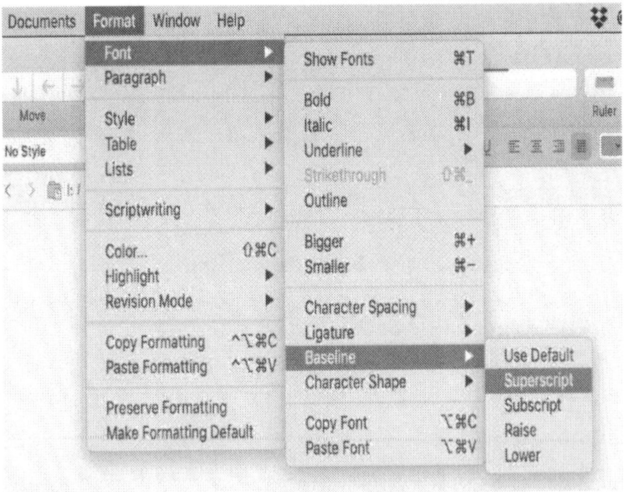

Figure 52: Changing Text Alignment in Scrivener 3

Additionally, choosing Paragraph from this menu allows you to choose many options including alignment, text direction and keeping your paragraphs together.

Sometimes, when you are writing a book to help other people you encounter something you've never used before. Such is the case with a feature under fonts called Ligature. Honestly, I was more familiar with the term as it is used in grisly crime novels – not so much with typography. However, Scrivener 3 has a function to adjust your ligature under Format ▸ Font ▸ Ligature. Being the curious former attorney that I am, even though I've never used this function, I set out to discover what it is. Basically, it refers to the way fonts appear and connect to each other. You can change this in Show Fonts (⌘T) by clicking the gear.

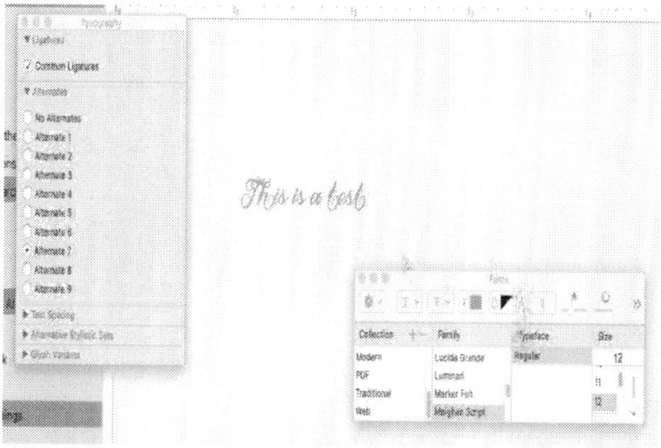

Figure 53: Ligatures in Scrivener 3

If you are working with a fancy font, there is a chance there are alternatives to each character type. That's what the ligature function is about. It allows you to choose different typography within the same font family.

One last note about formatting. Scrivener 3 has an option to Preserve Formatting under the Format menu. To use this feature, select the text you want to maintain special formatting – like for example if you changed the font to something fancy. Then click on Format ▸ Preserve Formatting. It will put a highlight box around the text you have selected. The purpose of this is to keep the special formatting visible in your output. Unfortunately, this only works some of the time. It typically works in Word documents and PDFs. However, it does not work when you are creating e-books. Additionally, make sure you can embed whatever font you choose to use. Otherwise, this feature won't work.

Revision Mode

Although it is not exactly the same as track changes in Microsoft Word, you can keep track of your revisions in Scrivener.

To use this tool, go to Format ▸ Revision Mode. After you have entered into this mode, you can assign a color to the changes you've made. You can change the colors available in the revision mode, however there doesn't seem to be a way to change the name of each mode. You may want to add a comment at the beginning of your manuscript which includes the key to your revision tasks. For example, you could make all points of view revisions a particular color and punctuation a different color, if you wish. Or, you can just make different rounds of revisions. Unlike text changes in Microsoft Word, using the revisions mode does not actually change your manuscript. It just allows you to keep track of your revisions.

Another way to track revisions is through in-line annotations. There is a setting in compile which allows you to disregard any comments and annotations in your final product.

Scrivener will continue to add text in a separate color until you exit from revision mode. To exit from revision mode, click None. Clicking on Remove All Revisions restores the text to its original color.

 Revision mode does not make corrections. It just helps you identify where they need to be made.

Now that we've discussed working with a manuscript in Scrivener 3, in the next chapter I will talk about some tools built into Scrivener 3 which will make producing a quality manuscript a little easier.

Speech to Text Capability

If you have the accessibility features turned on through your Mac's operating system, you can use the speech to text capability in Scrivener 3 to dictate your documents.

The speech to text engine included for free in the operating system of your Mac is not as accurate an external program like Dragon® Professional Individual 6.0.8. However, it is a usable program. Be aware it does not learn custom vocabulary words or learn from its mistakes. Even so, it can be a valuable tool (and it's free).

To access the speech to text capabilities within Scrivener, click on Edit ▸ Speech.

In a related function, you can have Scrivener read your text back to you. If you have set up the default keyboard shortcut for this function in your accessibility features on your operating system, pressing ⌥ and ESC will cause Mac's text to speech reader to read back your document. Although it might sound a little funny, it is a very helpful tool to catch punctuation and grammar errors in your manuscript. You can adjust the pitch and the speed of the voice used for read-back.

Chapter 6 – Tools to Improve Your Manuscript

It's hard to identify all the helpful side features in Scrivener 3. They are wide and varied. I'll address a few of them here.

Collections

Scrivener has many tools to assist your writing process.

The Collections feature is just one of them. This tool is great for determining internal consistency within your manuscript. For example, you may want to make a collection of chapters which follow a particular character to make sure the details are consistent all the way through your manuscript.

You could also make collections from the chapters you've already finished and the chapters you still have to work on. Collections can be made up of any variable you would like to include. If your project contains any collections, you can have them appear above your Binder by clicking the blue view button in the left-hand corner of your toolbar.

You can use tags you have added to your work such as labels, status or keywords to build your collections. To add files based on a search of these terms, you can bring up the search tool by using ⇧⌘F. Click on the magnifying glass and a list of options will appear. After your search results are created, you can click on the magnifying glass again and choose save search as a collection. Collections based on search results have a magnifying glass in front of the title. You can click the arrow next to the X and generate all the documents in the search in an editor window. You can work with a collection in any of the group modes including Scrivenings, corkboard and outline. If you add more files which meet the criteria of the search, just push this button again and it will be updated. By clicking on Binder order within your search, you can sort the contents of the search.

You can also create a collection by manually adding documents or files to a collection. A manually created collection does not have a magnifying glass in front of it, and the background is solid instead of striped. To create one, use the command key as you click on folders and documents you want to include. When you are finished, press the + next to the collections window. This will create a collection called new collection. If you want to change the title of this collection, click on it and type a new word. You can add and subtract files from this collection by dragging files into the collection and clicking the minus key to remove them.

After you are done working with your collections, you can hide the collections view by clicking on the blue view button in your toolbar.

Spell and Grammar Check

Scrivener offers both grammar and spell check tools. To access them, you can add an icon when you customize the toolbar or right-click on a word in your document. The grammar and spell check tools are an option on the menu that appears. Alternatively, you can also press ⌘: or ⌘; to start the spellcheck immediately. The spellcheck feature underlines misspelled words in red and grammar issues in green.

I'll be honest with you; I have a love/hate relationship with the spell and grammar check tool in Scrivener. In many ways, it is helpful. This is especially true for finding punctuation marks you have incorrectly used – for example if you forget to use a quotation mark at the end of dialogue. However, like many other spelling and grammar checking tools, the advice you receive can be incorrect. There are certain words it has a difficult time sorting through, including there and it's. Additionally, there is a tool tip which is supposed to appear when you click on an underlined word. However, it never seems to work properly for me. I must not have the magic touch with my mouse.

Even though I vastly prefer an external program called ProWritingAid (which incidentally works with Scrivener projects), I still use the spelling and grammar tools to help me clean up my writing as I draft my manuscript before I start my formal edit.

You can easily add words to the spell checker by clicking on a misspelled word and telling the spelling and grammar checker to learn a word. These settings are system wide, as the spellchecker relies on Mac's dictionary. If you need to eliminate a word you have added to the spellchecker, you can right click on it and choose Unlearn. Sometimes this may not work, so you can also edit any learned words by clicking on Automatic by Language ▸ Open Text Preferences in the Spelling and Grammar check window.

Name Generator

I don't know about you, but one of my biggest challenges in writing comes from the need to find names for my characters. When I first started writing, I couldn't imagine why this would be an issue. Now that I have written over thirty books, I understand the dilemma. Fortunately, Scrivener 3 has a tool to help with this problem.

If you choose Edit ▸ Writing Tools ▸ Name Generator, it will bring up a tool which allows you to search for names. You can set the complexity of the name you want and you can even add custom name dictionaries. When I first discovered that I could add custom name dictionaries, I searched the web to find some. Finding none, I discovered I could create my own by going to baby naming sites and choosing my own. I have since learned that Literature and Latte's community board has several lists available to create custom name dictionaries.

You can generate the names by gender and have the name generator try to add alliteration to the first and last name, use initials or add a middle name.

To add a custom dictionary, click on the + in the name generating tool. There are several name dictionaries available from the Literature and Latte website. You can create your own from genealogy or baby naming sites. Save the list of names as a .CSV file so you can import it.

Adding custom dictionaries to this tool makes it much more powerful. This is especially true if you are writing period specific fiction.

Linguistic Focus

Linguistic Focus is a simply named tool on the Edit menu under Writing Tools. (The keyboard shortcut is ^⌘L.) It's easy to overlook, however it is an extremely powerful tool and one of the best innovations included in Scrivener 3.

This little tool helps identify different areas of your writing. It helps with the editing process. In the example below, I have identified all the verbs in the scene I am working with.

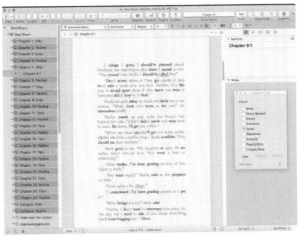

Figure 54: Linguistic Focus in Scrivener 3

The linguistic focus tool allows you to identify different parts of your document and fade the rest into the background. You can choose the amount of fade. At its most extreme setting, the only words visible on your page will be the words you highlight.

Imagine you decided to change the tense in your manuscript. Being able to identify all the verbs would be very helpful. Similarly, if you're trying to eliminate dialogue tags, highlighting all the dialogue will help speed up this process. If you are trying to eliminate the use of adverbs, the linguistic focus tool and Scrivener 3 can help you find them.

I am a big fan of this tool. However, unfortunately, you are limited to evaluating one file or document at a time.

Dictionary, Thesaurus and Other External Tools

You can easily link to a dictionary, thesaurus, Google and Wikipedia through Scrivener. Select a word or phrase in your manuscript and right-click. Choose writing tools from the menu and select one of the options. Opening these tools within Scrivener 3 is a particularly helpful option if you are trying to write distraction free. I don't know about the rest of you, but if I leave my work to go search for something on Google or Wikipedia, I get distracted and forget to get back to my writing. Accessing these tools through your Scrivener window cuts down on your chances of being distracted.

The dictionary Scrivener 3 uses depends on your system settings. If you need to change it for any reason, you can do so under Preferences ▸ Corrections ▸ System Text Preferences.

As you can see from the figure below, you can also set up a bunch of other options to make it easier to type or dictate your document. I am a fan of the automatic capitalization of sentences. When I'm tired, I often forget to capitalize the first word in a sentence.

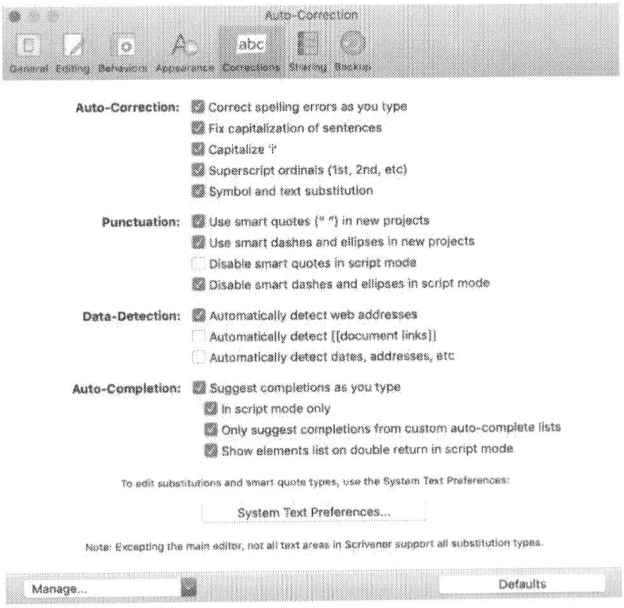

Figure 55: Correction Options Under Preferences in Scrivener 3

As an aside, one of my favorite language tools is a site called WordHippo.com. Unfortunately, I have not found a way to substitute this site for the existing thesaurus in Scrivener 3.

Substitutions, Transformations and Text Tidying Tools

The difference between a mediocre manuscript and one that looks polished can come down to the small details. Fortunately, Scrivener 3 has several tools to help you deal with the fussy minutia. These tools come in the form of substitutions, transformations and text tidying.

One of my favorite tools is the substitutions feature. This option on the edit menu allows you to substitute the type of quotes you use. I prefer to use curly quotes, but others do not. Scrivener gives you the option. You can also automatically format em dashes and ellipsis using substitutions.

There are many options under transformations. You can change the case of your text, convert your curly quotes to straight quotes and vice versa, and change the format of in-line annotations.

The tools under the text tidying menu are very helpful. You can delete tabs and multiple spaces project-wide among several other options. Zapping gremlins helps you remove unnecessary computer code which may cause your manuscript to glitch in certain places.

One of the other places you can perform rudimentary text cleanup functions is in the compile menu. You can click on the gear and remove hyperlinks, highlighting and leading spaces. There are other settings here too.

After my editor has finished working with my manuscript, I copy and paste each chapter back into Scrivener because I treat Scrivener files as master files. I find the Transformations tool under edit to be very handy. In Scrivener 3, they introduced a feature to remove small caps. It makes me want to do cartwheels because it makes it easy for me to remove small caps.

Now that we've discussed how to create a manuscript and how to use tools to make it better, I'm going to talk about tools to search your manuscript.

Chapter 7 – The Art of the Search

Aside from the new compiling tool, the single most improved feature in Scrivener 3 is its enhanced abilities to search. The quick search bar is one of my favorite tools. In this section, we will discuss both the new quick search feature and the regular search feature – including project search and replace.

Quick Search

Unlike a standard project search, quick search brings up the first ten incidents of a word or phrase. This makes correcting errors during the editing process so much easier. For example, one of my proofreaders goes through my documents and finds the mistakes. When she identifies them for me, she lists a few of the surrounding words. With the new quick search feature, I can just plug those into the quick search bar and come up with the precise location of the error. Personally, I believe this one feature alone is enough to warrant an upgrade from Scrivener 1 or 2.

As I stated earlier, if you have entered progress targets into your project, the quick search bar will show both your overall progress and your daily progress. The immediate accessibility of this visual aid is a powerful motivator for me. The colors of the bar on top changes depending upon how far you have progressed in your project. The default colors for this are red, yellow and green. Although you can, as I have, assign your own color scheme. This is done in the preferences window.

Although I love the new quick search tool, it has some limitations. For example:

It only shows the first ten search results in context. If you need to search more than the first ten, you must click on Full Project Search which brings you to the traditional search results.

Still, if you can search with a few words or a phrase, this feature is spectacularly helpful, even with its limitations.

Sometimes, the quick search tool is not robust enough and you will need to do a full project search using Search in Project.

Search in Project

Users of earlier versions of Scrivener will no doubt recognize Search in Project. You can access this tool by clicking the magnifying glass on your toolbar or by clicking Edit ▸ Find ▸ Search in Project. The keyboard shortcut for this feature is ⇧⌘F.

Although the Search in Project function is powerful and can be customized to include specific files, documents or collections, it has limitations. Unlike Quick Search, the program does not lead you directly to the word you searched for. Instead, it simply highlights the search words in each folder or document. You can manually search for the highlighted words. If you have a long document, this can take a substantial amount of time.

Fortunately, Scrivener does have a way to make this process a little less painful using the Find feature (⌘F). After you have clicked on the magnifying glass in the toolbar, it will bring a list of the folders or documents in your binder which contain the words you have searched for. Place your cursor on the list, and press ⌘A to select the whole list. Then, press ⌘F to bring up the find box. If you choose next, Scrivener will toggle through and highlight each incident of the word in the search results. This approach is faster than manually searching for each search result.

You can place limits on what files Search in Project examines. You can search the whole project, documents within the project, or for specific formatting by clicking the arrow beside the magnifying glass in the toolbar.

If your search ever produces unexpected results, check to see if you have applied a search filter here.

When I am writing fiction, I have a list of words I always remove before sending my work to beta readers or my editor. When I search for these words, I will frequently limit the scope of the search to a chapter or a small group of chapters so I don't become overwhelmed by the editing task.

 If you use Search in Project and you have a difficult time seeing the highlighted words, remember, you can always change the color of the highlight in preferences.

Personally, I like to assign a neon color to the highlight so it's easy to locate in a long document.

Project Replace

Project Replace is a powerful tool. Because I use voice recognition software, I use this tool frequently to remove extra spaces placed in my document by Dragon® Professional Individual 6.0.8. However, it's also a great tool for changing a character's name midstream or when you are modifying a previous project for your new project.

Project Replace does exactly what it says. It searches your whole project for a particular word or character and replaces them with something else. Always double check your input into this tool because you cannot undo the changes made when you use this tool. Trust me, making a mistake here can be catastrophic. One time, I was trying to replace two spaces with one space and somehow I got distracted and forgot to put the space in the replace box. Every place I had two spaces in my document now had no spaces. It took a long time to re-edit my document after my oversight.

The Project Replace tool is customizable, you can tell it to search and ignore capitalization and you can choose which items the function affects. For example, if you don't want the changes you made to affect your Snapshot or your synopsis, you can simply uncheck those options. In fact, I recommend not including your Snapshot in Project Replace. Additionally, I recommend taking a Snapshot before doing anything which can impact your entire document.

Chapter 8 –An In-Depth Look at the Binder

As I've said several times, the Binder is the backbone of your project in Scrivener. It gives you an overview of your document and allows you to move information around without copying and pasting. The philosophy behind Scrivener is to allow authors to write however they feel comfortable. Aside from the mandatory files in Scrivener – the Draft Folder, the Research Folder and trash, all other entries into your Binder are entirely up to your discretion.

If you are the type of author who likes to write all your thoughts at once with no structure, Scrivener can accommodate that. Conversely, if you prefer to divide your manuscript up into many scenes of varying degrees of detail, Scrivener can work with attitude.

At the heart of this flexibility is the Binder. You are no longer confined to writing chronologically and all of your information, manuscript and resources can be kept in one location. So, if you typically write your scenes in separate documents in a word processor like Microsoft Word and then try to copy and paste them into a coherent document when you have finished your manuscript, you will find Scrivener much easier to work with. Scrivener 3 does this work for you.

In this chapter, I'll share some tips to make it easier to work with the Binder.

Working with Files

In Scrivener, your manuscript folders go into your Draft Folder. This folder may be named something different depending upon the template you started with. In some, it's called manuscript or screenplay. Whatever it's called in your project, your writing goes in the top folder in your Binder.

If you are using a Scrivener template, Scrivener places a help file in the top folder of each template. It summarizes the features of each individual template. I urge you to take a few moments to read it. These tip sheets give a lot of helpful information about special features in each individual template. These templates are often customized to meet specific needs with title pages, style guides, character and plot sheets as well as demonstration projects.

There are several ways to insert a new file or document into your Binder. You can click on the big green + in the toolbar, or, you can click on the folder with the + in the footer status bar, or you can add it under Project in the menu, or you can right-click on an existing folder in your Binder and click on add. The keyboard shortcut ⌥⌘N will also create a new folder.

When you add a folder to Scrivener, it will have new folder as the default name. You can change this by clicking in your synopsis or on the name of the file itself in the Binder.

For most purposes, it does not matter whether you add documents or folders in Scrivener 3. There are slight differences in the visibility of sub-folders in your editing window and the default scene separators. Other than that, they function remarkably the same.

Scrivener makes it easy to tell what type of content is in a file or document by its appearance. The mandatory folders have their own specific icons and if you add new files or documents to your project, the appearance of these will vary.

If you enjoy working on sections of your manuscript out of order, it is simple to tell which files have content and sub-folders. In the graphic below, I have shown eight levels of folders. I could have continued to add more levels had I chosen to. This graphic is just to illustrate the different folder icons based on the content within them.

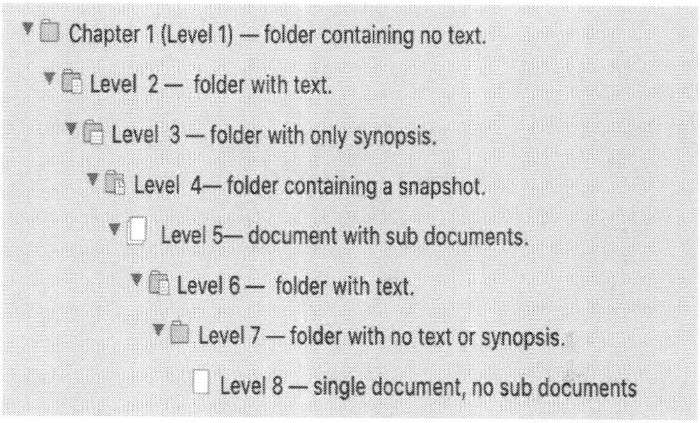

▼ 📁 Chapter 1 (Level 1) — folder containing no text.
  ▼ 📁 Level 2 — folder with text.
    ▼ 📁 Level 3 — folder with only synopsis.
      ▼ 📁 Level 4 — folder containing a snapshot.
        ▼ 📄 Level 5 — document with sub documents.
          ▼ 📁 Level 6 — folder with text.
            ▼ 📁 Level 7 — folder with no text or synopsis.
              📄 Level 8 — single document, no sub documents

Figure 56: Types of Folders Within Scrivener 3 and the Icons Which Represent Them Based on Content

The different levels of files is not only aesthetically pleasing as you navigate through your document, they come into play later on when you are assigning Section Types. You can elect to assign Section Types to your files or documents differently depending on the level in your Binder.

In my opinion, the easiest way to change the level of a file or document in your Binder is to use the Move button. It has arrow key icons which you can add to your toolbar. Alternatively, you can click and drag a folder or document to another location in your Binder or to a different level. There are several keyboard shortcuts which move the level of your folders or documents.

- **Edit ▸ Move ▸ Move Down** ^⌘↓
- **Edit ▸ Move ▸ Move Left** ^⌘←
- **Edit ▸ Move ▸ Move Right** ^⌘→
- **Edit ▸ Move ▸ Move Up** ^⌘↑

I move files quite a bit when I am editing. Sometimes, a chapter works better with the scenes in a different order.

To make it easier for you to differentiate your folders in a project, you can change the icon without changing the file type. To do this, right-click on the folder or document and choose change icon. If Scrivener 3's selection is not to your liking, you can add your own icon files through manage custom icons on the custom icon menu.

The ability to change the icon on each folder can be helpful. I use this feature when I want to mark where I have left off in my Binder. I right-click on the document in question and then change the icon to a star. The next time I open this project, I'll know exactly where I left off because the folder will now have a star beside the name instead of the file.

If you are anything like me, many of your manuscripts have common elements between them. This could be your copyright page, your backlist, or your author information. Additionally, you could have a story bible, plot sheets, character sheets or location sheets applicable to multiple documents.

Scrivener 3 makes sharing files between projects easy. You can select multiple files using the command key and then right clicking on one of the folders while holding down the ⌘. This will bring up a menu which gives you the option to copy your files to another project. One caveat: the project you want to receive the files must also be open in Scrivener.

One of my favorite ways to move folders between documents is to highlight them and drag them between projects. To do this, make sure your projects are open in separate windows and click on the green button in the upper left-hand side of the screen to make your window smaller. Then, click on the window menu and choose float window. After you have done this, you can have two documents open in Scrivener at the same time. Select the files you want to move to the other file and then just click and drag those files to the Binder in the new project. You can move multiple files at once as long as they are selected in the Binder of your donor document.

If you are moving files with the same name, make sure you move the old files to the trash first.

For example, if I am updating an old book list with new information, I need to throw away the old files which contain my book list before dragging the new ones in. Failure to do this can cause confusion. I know this from personal experience. Trust me, save yourself the hassle. You can always drag the old files out of the Trash Folder if you change your mind.

If you have a document or file within your Binder that has been set up the way you prefer to work, you can duplicate the folder and its sub-folders by using ⌘D. If you want to duplicate the folder without sub-folders, you can press ⇧⌘D.

Don't forget, you can change the appearance of a folder in your Binder with your label colors. I use this feature a lot because I write novels with dual points of view. It is easier for me to keep track of whose voice I'm writing in if I assign each character a specific label color. I frequently work with multiple projects at once. So, I try to make certain my character label colors are completely different.

The Power of the Right-Click

I know it seems silly to give a function like right-click its own section. However, I want to highlight this simple solution so you remember it exists. The right-click menus in Scrivener will help you navigate more efficiently. Each mode in the group mode has its own contextual menus which come up when you right-click.

If you right-click on any file in the Binder, a menu will pop up with several popular options for working with your manuscript. This is usually how I assign Section Types or change the status of my files.

 Right-clicking after you've selected folders or documents in your binder allows you to copy those files to another project. Make sure you have the second project open when you try to use this tool.

The right-click function is context dependent. For example, it won't let you delete your Draft Folder and if you click on the Trash Folder, you will have the opportunity to empty your trash. (I don't recommend emptying your trash until you are completely finished with your project.)

Keep in mind that you can use the right-click function to add folders to your bookmarks. So, if you have details in one chapter you need to refer back to when writing another, you can just bookmark one file to the folder you are working with. This is also a good way to work with your story bible or character sheets if you have them in your Research Folder.

If you like to navigate between documents in your project with links, you may find the Copy Document Link function helpful. It can be reached by right clicking anywhere on the Binder and navigating to the bottom of the menu which pops up.

Odds and Ends

We've talked extensively about using keyboard shortcuts or the toolbar icons with the blue arrows to move your files within the Binder. However, there is another way to move your folders up and down the Binder. You can click and drag them where you need them. A blue line will appear where Scrivener plans to put your folders or documents. You can pull it to the left and right to determine where it goes in the hierarchy.

If you write with multiple editors open, you might find the Binder Selection settings helpful. You can choose whether to have Scrivener navigate to the same place in both editor windows. Personally, I like the fact that in Scrivener if I make a selection in one view it automatically makes the same selection in the other editing window. For me, it helps ensure that I am working in the same document. However, other people may not like this feature so much. Fortunately, like most everything else, Scrivener 3 allows you to choose how to use its features.

This feature is located under the Navigate menu. Unless you have more than one editor window open, the Binder Selection choices will be grayed out. If you want Scrivener to select the same folder or file in both windows, you can click on the both windows option. If you are editing and need to have your entire file structure available in the outline or Corkboard Mode, set this feature to change only the current editor.

You can use Scrivener to automatically generate a table of contents. Although, be careful not to duplicate this in your compile settings or you will have two.

If you are compiling to an e-book format, there will be an additional icon on the top left-hand side of the Compile Pane which allows you to set your preferences. If you don't want to add a table of contents here, you can uncheck the boxes in this menu.

If you do not want your sub-folders to be in your manually generated table of contents, collapse them in your Binder before you create a table of contents document.

To create your own table of contents, add a new document or folder where you want the table of contents to be. Then, name the file Contents or Table of Contents. Next, choose the files or documents you want to be featured in the table of contents. Don't forget to include your front and back matter if you want them listed in the table of contents. After everything is highlighted in your Binder, click on Edit ▸ Copy Special ▸ Copy as TOC. Go to the folder you created and paste the contents of your clipboard into your Scrivenings window. When this is done, you can format your table of contents however you wish using scriveners formatting tools.

 A manually entered table of contents is a static document. If you change the order of your chapters in your Binder, you need to find the table of contents you created and go through the steps again to update it.

Do you have an overwhelmingly long or complex binder? Many authors I know choose to use one project for an entire series. This can create a daunting binder. However, Scrivener 3 for Windows has included a tool to deal with this. It is called Hoist Binder. This function allows you to essentially zoom in on a folder within your binder. Simply click on the file in the binder you want to use and choose View ▸ Outline ▸ Hoist Binder. After you've done this, all the folders in your binder are hidden except for the one you selected and its subfolders. When you want to go back to viewing your entire binder, choose View ▸ Outline ▸ Unhoist Binder.

If you would like to know how many subfolders are in each folder or document in your binder, you can choose to show that number. Go to View ▸ Outline ▸ Show Subdocuments in Binder.

Now that we've discussed the Binder in greater detail, I'll move on to discussing Scrivenings.

Chapter 9 – Mastering Scrivenings

Scrivenings is one editing mode within group modes. It is just a fancy way to refer to the portion of Scrivener which looks like a word processor.

In many ways, the Scrivenings section functions just like a traditional word processor. However, unlike traditional word processors, the way you view the Scrivenings pane doesn't need to have anything to do with how the final outlook appears. For example, you may write in hot pink Comic Sans just for fun, but your output in the compiler can be a nice, sedate Times New Roman.

In the Scrivenings window, you can use the highlight tool and format the text different colors to show areas you need to edit or different character points of view. When you compile, you can choose not to show your font colors or highlights.

Remember, if you want to type or dictate in a distraction free environment, you can use the compose mode. If you turn on typewriter scrolling, the cursor will stay in the same spot as you continue to write or dictate.

If you want your document to appear as it might when it is compiled, you can set the styles to resemble your settings in the format compile window and choose page view. Just make sure you set up the proper page size and margins under File ▸ Page Setup first.

Right-clicking while you are in Scrivenings, will bring up a contextual menu. One option on this menu is to split your document. If you select some existing text, it will become the name of the folder Scrivener 3 creates.

You can monitor your word count and progress toward any targets you have set in the Footer Status Bar in the Scrivenings mode. You can navigate between pages by clicking on the piece of paper or the arrows on either side in the footer status bar. If the paper is checked beside your target, it means it has been selected to be included in your compile settings.

There are some features available in Scrivener 3 which I didn't discuss in-depth earlier. One of these involves using pictures in your Draft Folder.

Working with Images

I frequently insert pictures into my manuscript (particularly when I write nonfiction).

 Scrivener 3 is structured in a way that prevents you from directly dragging a picture into your Draft Folder.

Typically, pictures are restricted to the Research Folder. However, if you use Insert Image From File, you can place an image file in your manuscript. You can also use a link to an external source.

 Using a link to a file instead of an actual image may be helpful if you don't have the final image for your document.

The link just acts as a placeholder. However, for your final manuscript, you may want to insert the pictures into your manuscript since you may not control access to the files on an external server. Once you have added an image to Scrivener, you can click on it and resize it and adjust its resolution and the title of the picture. Unfortunately, in Scrivener you cannot wrap text around your image. If you want the image in your manuscript to include wrapped text, you'll need to compile your document to be edited in a different program like InDesign or Microsoft Word.

There is an option if you right-click while you are using Scrivenings to import a picture from a camera or a scanner.

Be aware that adding images to your Scrivener file will increase your file size. Depending upon which royalty plan you use to list your books on Amazon, using images may significantly reduce the royalties owed to you.

Just as an aside, if you are writing a manuscript which includes screenshots, the resolution of your screenshots depends on your monitor. Set your monitor to the highest resolution possible.

In the compiler, you can have Scrivener resize your images depending upon your output. This is very helpful when you are compiling to Microsoft Word. It saves you time in preparing your manuscript for printing. You can alter the DPI with this setting too.

If you plan to use images as your section breaks, they need to be placed in your Binder. These images go in the research section. Click and drag them from the Finder window on your Mac. The rest of the work will be done during the compiling process. I will discuss using custom section breaks in Chapter 12.

Adding Math Equations

Sometimes, functions in Scrivener 3 need an outside program to be utilized. Such is the case with math equations.

You can insert math equations into Scrivener 3. However, you need an external program called Math Type. This is a subscription-based service that costs around fifty dollars a year. However, if you write textbooks or research papers which frequently feature math questions, it might be worth the expense.

Working with Tables

You can use tables within Scrivener. They work much the same way as tables in other word processing programs. (Although, there are fewer options for changing the appearance of the tables.) If you are working with the table, the right click menu becomes contextual in Scrivenings and will bring up several options related specifically to tables, including the option to remove the table and restore the text to normal.

Keep in mind when using tables in e-books, every device displays e-books differently, and readers may have their own choice of font and line spacing. Therefore, your table may not appear as you expected. If you need your table to remain unchanged by the reader, you need to save your table as a picture. However, make sure the picture is small enough to fit on one page. Most e-readers don't cope very well with pictures that need to span more than one page.

I work almost exclusively in the Scrivenings pane, however there are other views. Next, I will talk about working with the Corkboard Mode.

Chapter 10 – Working with the Corkboard

If you love working with sticky notes and index cards, the Corkboard Mode may be the perfect solution for you. It's like a virtual bulletin board which allows you to manipulate your files without having to use copy and paste.

In this mode, you can easily write a synopsis for each section of your book or work with the synopsis automatically generated by auto fill. Additionally, you can move files around in the Corkboard Mode before committing them to your Binder by working in free-form mode.

In this section, I'll discuss this unique view and how to incorporate it into your workflow.

Manipulating Index Cards

The way you work with index cards has been upgraded and expanded in Scrivener 3. You can still work with them the traditional way with each card presented in order from side to side or top to bottom. By choosing the top layer of any nested folders or documents in your Binder and switching to Corkboard Mode, you can see all the folders underneath the folder or document you selected. If you see a stack of index cards on your corkboard, that means another level of documents or files exists. To make these appear, just click on the icon on the index card. To further customize your index cards, you can add a status stamp by pressing ^⌘S, or you can show labels ^⌘P or keywords ^⌘K.

A synopsis generated from the first few words of your document or file may appear on the index card. However, as soon as you type over that information with a new synopsis, it will appear in black. This synopsis will carry over to your outline and the Inspector in your Binder.

You can click on and drag the index cards to change the order in which they appear. However, unless you are in free-form mode, any changes you make in the order of your index cards will appear in your Binder.

If you want to try out an arrangement of your index cards without it affecting your Binder, you need to be in free-form. To enter free-form mode click on the free-form option on your footer status bar. When you are in free-form mode, the word Commit will appear by the free-form button. When you are ready to change your Binder, just click this button.

Scrivener 3 has added a new powerful view called Arrange by Label. You can have your cards follow a horizontal or vertical line. This is helpful when you assign labels for points of view, discrete periods of time, or to specific characters. By visually seeing your chapters follow a particular line, you can more easily determine if your chapters are balanced in terms of point of view or if each character has enough chapters for the role they play in your story. Below is an example of using Arrange by Label in a romance novel I wrote which contained several points of view.

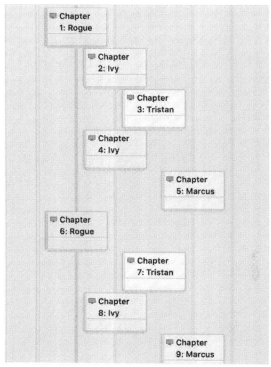

Figure 57: Arrange by Label in Scrivener 3

When using the Arrange by Label view, you can change the label on a particular card by dragging it to a different line. This will change the label and the Inspector, the Outline Mode and when you use the compiler.

As with files, you can use the ⌘ while you click on index cards to select multiple cards. Once you have selected multiple cards, you can move them around your corkboard or copy them to another project by right clicking on the corkboard and choosing Copy to Project.

In addition to moving index cards around on your corkboard, you can change the appearance of the cards themselves.

Changing the Appearance of Your Corkboard

You can change the appearance of your index cards by clicking on Scrivener ▸ Preferences ▸ Appearance. Then, in the left panel select Corkboard. Personally, I find the font in the index cards a little difficult to see. Therefore, I always enlarge the font. You can also change the way your index card appears by adding lines or rounded corners. If you are used to the color pins from earlier versions, they have been replaced with the ability to use labels and keywords.

You can adjust the appearance of the index cards by clicking on the four index cards in the lower right-hand corner of the Footer Status Bar while you are in Corkboard Mode. This setting will allow you to change the number of cards that appear in a row and the size of the index cards. Additionally, you can check the box so that your cards scale up and down in proportion to the size of your Scrivener 3 window.

Labels and Keywords

Labels and keywords really shine in the Corkboard Mode. You can set the properties of labels to change the entire color of the index cards or, you can have the label color show up on the edge. As I've mentioned before, labels are incredibly flexible. You can track point of view, plot lines, beats, locations and timelines by using labels or keywords. You can customize both the labels and the keywords to match your needs. Keywords will appear as little chips on the edge of your index card. Unlike labels, you can assign multiple keywords to a single chapter. With labels you can use only one.

I would be remiss if I didn't talk about assigning a status to your cards. For example, you can indicate that you are in the third round of revisions or that you've already checked a chapter with a grammar checker. By pressing ^⌘S you can make your status appear across your cards. You can set the opacity of this stamp under Preferences (⌘,). Status stamps can give you an overview of your project in one simple glance.

The corkboard and index cards are a handy way to look at your project. However, sometimes they don't contain enough information. For that, the Outline Mode is a good alternative. We will talk about the Outline Mode in the next chapter.

Chapter 11 – Drilling Down the Outline

There are some modes Scrivener I don't utilize as often as others and I forget how helpful they are. The Outline Mode is one of those views for me. After all, I am a dyed-in-the wool pantser. However, I occasionally like to work in the Outline Mode because it helps me get an overall picture of my whole document, lets me see if chapters are unbalanced, and discover plot holes. I like to show the number of words in each chapter and scene. That way, I can see if a scene is dragging on and may need to be divided. Conversely, I can also see if a particular chapter is exceptionally light on content. Additionally, I can see the flow of a document from start to finish.

In this chapter, I'm going to give you some tips on how to customize your outline and navigate through it. Finally, I'll discuss ways to print your outline.

Navigating in the Outline

As we talk about the Outline Mode, it is important to remember that you need to select a level in your outline which has sub-folders in order for the outlining feature to work. Generally, when I work in the outline, I work from the highest level in my Binder. This view allows me to see my entire document in outline form. Much like the Binder, if you don't want to see every sub-folder, you can collapse each level by clicking on the little arrow next to the title of your document or by using the following keyboard shortcuts:

View ▸ Outline ▸ Collapse All ⌘0
View ▸ Outline ▸ Expand All ⌘9
View ▸ Outline ▸ Next Container ⌃⌥↓
View ▸ Outline ▸ Previous Container ⌃⌥↑

Interestingly, the Outline Mode functions a little bit like a spreadsheet. You can sort each column A to Z or biggest to smallest and vice versa. Sorting the columns in Outline Mode does not affect your Binder or manuscript.

You can add new files or documents to your outline just like you would in your Binder or

Corkboard Mode. The + adds a document and the + in the folder as a new folder. As in the Binder, you can change the hierarchy of a document or folder in your outline by using the blue arrow keys you may have placed in your toolbar or ^⌘ with the arrow keys. This works to move your folders or documents up and down your outline.

Any changes made to status, keywords, or labels will be updated in the Binder, Corkboard and the Inspector.

Customizing Your Outline

You can customize your outline to include the columns you need to see. For example, you can look at labels, keywords, status, targets, and the date the document was created or modified.

To choose these columns, just click on the arrow next to the Inspector in your header status bar. You can even add custom columns by using the Metadata in your Inspector. You can change your Metadata and add categories by clicking on the icon that looks like a price tag in your Inspector or by clicking on custom columns under the list of options for the outline.

You can reorganize the order in which Scrivener presents your columns by clicking and dragging the columns to your desired location.

Labels and Keywords

Labels and keywords can be helpful when you're working in the Outline Mode. They are also very flexible and may be used for a variety of things.

For example, if you are a fan of using beats such as *Romancing the Beat* by Gwen Hayes or *Save the Cat* by Blake Snyder, you can assign each type of beat a different color label or keyword and add those values to your outline. If you use a label, the color of the label will go clear across the line in your outline. If you use a keyword instead, it will show up as a small color block in the keyword column. You can only assign one label per document or folder. However, you can assign several keywords. For example, you could use keywords to track time, location, character interactions or point of view.

Printing Your Outline

It's not intuitive, but you can print your outline as it appears in Scrivener 3. First, in the outline pane, make sure you are on a level which allows you to see all the parts of the outline you would like to print. Then go to page setup under the file menu or ⇧⌘P. A window will appear with margin settings etc. Click on the down arrow beside page attributes. It will change the selection in this box to Scrivener. Once you are in this menu, choose outlines. This will give you a menu which will allow you to choose which information in your outline you would like to print. When you are done choosing, click OK to close the window.

Next, go to File ▸ Print Current document (or ⌘P). This will bring up a typical print screen. From that, you can either print it out on a regular printer or save it as a PDF.

This is a good method to print out your outline if you just want a quick copy. It's not fancy, but it works.

Another option for printing your manuscript as an outline is to use the compile feature and choose one of the many outline formats available. To work with this successfully, you may have to create more Section Types in your document and apply them appropriately to match the outline formats in Scrivener 3. The list of available Section Types is listed in the middle pane under the Section Layout Pane. If you need to add more sections to your project to work with an outline format, go to Project ▸ than Project Settings (or press ⌥⌘,). After you have assigned the appropriate Section Types, choose the folders you want to include in your outline and press compile.

If you want to work with your outline in other formats, you can export your outline to a .CSV file by clicking File ▸ Export ▸ Outline Contents as .CSV. After you open your .CSV file in Microsoft

Excel, you can convert it to a Microsoft Word document.

Now that you've learned about the Binder, Scrivenings, the Corkboard and Outline Mode, we can now talk about ways to output your document with the Compiler.

Chapter 12 – Demystifying Compile

When I told people I was going to write this book, many authors confessed to me that they only use Scrivener 3 as a word processing program and organizational tool because they find compiling too daunting.

It makes me sad when I hear something like that, because – although it takes time to learn – compile is one of the most powerful features in Scrivener 3. In my opinion, the compile feature is one thing that sets Scrivener 3 apart from other applications in which you could write your story. The compile feature gives you control over the formatting and the method of output.

I know many people prefer the simplicity of a program like Vellum. However, because the makers of Vellum had to make their program easy to use under all circumstances, they had to eliminate some flexibility and options. I own Vellum, but I only use it to create large print books. I have formatted my own books for years using Scrivener. (Yes, even in Scrivener for Windows.) You can make professional, unique looking documents with Scrivener. The number of ways you can compile your manuscript without making any changes to it is astonishing. Of all the ways to output a document and compile, I've only used about four. I routinely compile into Microsoft Word – where I do my finish formatting to remove things like widows and orphans and make tiny adjustments to spacing. I now use .EPUB files to upload my manuscript to Amazon instead of .MOBI files. I have also compiled to a PDF and have compiled obscure files for NaNoWriMo.

 If you are writing for NaNoWriMo and want to keep the contents of your manuscript secret while you validate your word count, output it as a .txt file and pick NaNoWriMo Obfuscated as your format type. This will produce a scrambled manuscript with your word count represented.

The options available for compiling and formatting compelling documents in Scrivener 3 are vast and limited only by your imagination.

First, I'm going to talk about choosing an output method in the compiler.

Output Method

Using the same manuscript to produce files in different formats is one of my favorite features in Scrivener. Without making direct changes to a manuscript, you can produce a paperback or an e-book and virtually everything in between.

Like many other things in Scrivener, the choices are dynamic. So, if you create a PDF, the formatting options which appear in the Format Pane will differ from the ones presented to create a text document.

Step one in the compiling process is to choose the output of your document. However, before you even get to the compiling stage, I recommend that you click on File ▸ Page Setup and choose your page size and margins. If you don't see the size you want to use, you can make a custom size and give it a name. For example, I recently changed my trim size to 5.5×8.5 and I had to set up a new paper size. I'm so creative I named it new series size. If you click on the box that says page attributes, you will be presented with a Scrivener option. If you click on that, you can set up margins.

After you have chosen all of your page

attributes and set your margins, now you are ready to complete step one of the compile process and choose your output. To bring up the compile menu, you can choose it from your toolbar, find it under File ‣ Compile (or press ⌥⌘E). Output options are roughly grouped together by file type. For example, all the output methods that produce an e-book are together.

Just a side note - I used to produce .MOBI files using the KindleGen tool from Amazon https://www.amazon.com/gp/feature.html?ie=UTF8&docId=1000765211

After much experimentation, I have determined this is an unnecessary added step. An .EPUB file does not display any differently or increase your delivery charge.

However, if you are more comfortable using .MOBI files with Amazon, you can download the KindleGen tool and use it with Scrivener 3. The first time you use the MOBI output on a project, Scrivener 3 for Windows will warn you that you don't have KindleGen and provide a link. Download the file and place it in a location where you can find it. A permanent location on your hard drive is best. Then, when you set up to compile your .MOBI, you'll be instructed to tell Scrivener where the file is located by using the Choose button.

After you choose the output method, the next move will seem a little counterintuitive. Head over to the Compile Pane.

Compile Pane

The Compile Pane has a list of files on the left-hand side of the window when you choose compile. This is how you tell Scrivener which files you want to include in your final product. Although it's relatively straight-forward, there are some things you need to watch for.

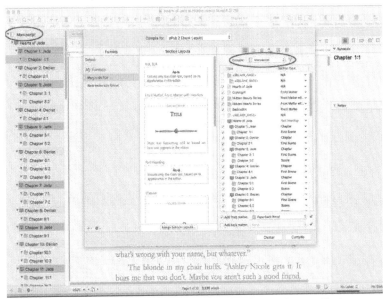

Figure 58: Selecting Files to Include in Compile in Scrivener 3

In the example above, I have circled the highest level in my Binder. In this case, it happens to be Manuscript. Whenever possible, this should be the level you compile.

If you have more than one copy of your manuscript in your Draft Folder, it is a good practice to drag the copy you are not using into your Research Folder to avoid confusion.

See the little funnel icon next to the files you want to include? It is actually a filter which allows you to exclude documents.

Be careful not to inadvertently filter the files included in the compiler.

As with many cautionary tales in this book, this one was inspired by true life events. Somehow, I had accidentally applied a filter. I wasn't aware of this setting, and it took me forever to come up with a solution.

Now that you have the proper file identified and new filters attached, you can choose which files or documents you want included in your document.

You can check these all at once or press down the ⌥ while you click one of the check boxes. This will select all the documents. If you want just a few removed, you can press the command key while you are clicking in a box you have selected to unselect it.

Using my novel as an example, I'll tell you some of my selections and why I make them. I often sell my books at in-person events where I inscribe them. Therefore, I like to have a blank page before my title page. When I am compiling into Microsoft Word, I add two extra blank pages at the beginning before my title page and one blank page after my dedication. I do not select the file which contains the name of my book.

I happen to use the same front material for my paperbacks and my e-books. So, in this example, the Add Front Matter says Paperback Novel. However, you definitely don't need to do it this way. You could add different front and back matter depending on the output and the final destination of your manuscript. For example, if you are posting e-books, you might want to have a separate back matter for the ones which contain Amazon links and create a separate front and back matter section for the e-books you post elsewhere which don't have Amazon specific links.

There is a little lock beside the front and back matter sections in the compiler. If you click on the locks, the front and back matter you have selected will remain consistent every time you use that output method.

After you've chosen which files or documents you want to include in your output, next is a good idea to make sure your Section Types have been chosen correctly. If you find one that's wrong or unassigned, you can click on the down arrow and choose the proper type.

You might notice that there are icons across the top of the Compile Pane. Much like the Inspector, each one has an individual purpose.

The first one, which looks like a list, displays which documents or files you want to include in your output. It also allows you to assign front and back matter folders (which reside in your Research Folder in the Binder). Finally, you can assign Section Types from this window.

The next icon represents Metadata. This is where you put your title and author information. Depending upon how you set up Scrivener, this may or may not be pre-populated.

 Always check your Metadata settings – even if you think you've Included the correct information.

I once published a book with the wrong title on every other page. I used a template created from another project and forgot to change the Metadata. Don't make my mistake – It's more than a little embarrassing.

You also have the option to add subjects and keywords here. Personally, I don't recommend it since your marketing strategies may change over time and it's easy to forget about this setting.

The next icon is the gear. Clicking on this will allow you to change many settings from whether you include the text color, highlighting, in-line annotations and footnotes, among others. These options will change depending on the output method you have chosen. One of the handiest settings here is the option to remove white trailing spaces.

I adjust my settings in this window depending on which output I am using. For example, if I am compiling books to use as paperbacks, I remove all the hyperlinks. Additionally, I increase the DPI so that my pictures print well.

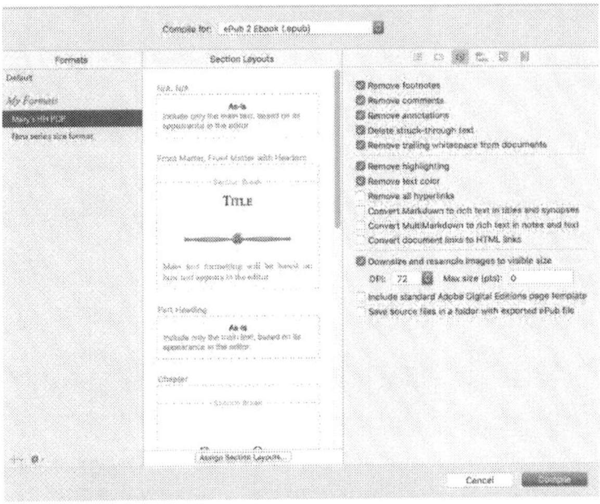

Figure 59: Optional Settings Under Compile in Scrivener 3

The next icon represents replacements. This feature will allow you to identify things you want replaced in your output. For example, if you have written a document for NaNoWriMo and avoided using contractions to increase your word count, you can set Scrivener to replace did not with didn't or you are with you're. Additionally, this feature is helpful when you are working with words with accent marks. So, you can type the word in your document without accent marks, but use the replace feature to substitute a more complex version using the proper accents.

The next icon only appears when you're working with e-books. It looks like a picture because it is where you add your cover photo. If you want to use a cover on your e-book file, you need to drag your cover into the research section of the Binder. For consistency, I always place mine right above my front matter folder.

The final icon may or may not appear depending upon your output selection. This icon allows you to set parameters for your table of contents in an e-book. You can choose what the section is called and how it appears. If you have already added a table of contents manually (as described in Chapter 8), unselect the boxes in this menu.

After you have chosen all of your folders or documents, set section layouts and adjusted your advanced settings, it is now time for you to move to the Format Pane.

Format Pane

As I described before, if the output method is equivalent to telling the print setter what you would like to create and the Compile Pane is telling the printer what you would like included in the final product, the Format Pane is equivalent to telling the printer what you would like your work to look like.

The Formats offered to you depend on the output method you choose. For example, there will be several more options for a .PDF document than there are for a simple text document.

Scrivener comes pre-populated with Formats to match your output. However, if none of those work for your project, you can adapt the existing Formats to suit your preferences.

You also have the option to create a Format from scratch. Personally, I find it easier to adapt an existing Format which is close, but not perfect for my project.

You can preview what each Format will look like when applied to Section Types in the Section Layout Pane. If you like how it appears, perfect! You are ready to move on to the next step. However, if you want to change things like spacing or font choice, you'll have to edit an existing Format or create your own from scratch.

To edit an existing Format, right click on the Format's name. Then choose Edit or Duplicate and Edit.

 When modifying Formats, I strongly recommend you choose Duplicate and Edit, rather than changing the original Format.

When you click on this, you will be asked to save the Format under a new name. At this point, you have two options. You can save the Format under My Formats and it will be saved globally. Every project you create in Scrivener 3 will have the option to use this format. Conversely, you can save it under Project Formats and it will be available to that specific project.

 The benefit to saving a format as a Project Format is that it attaches to your Scrivener file and other people who open your file will have access to the Format.

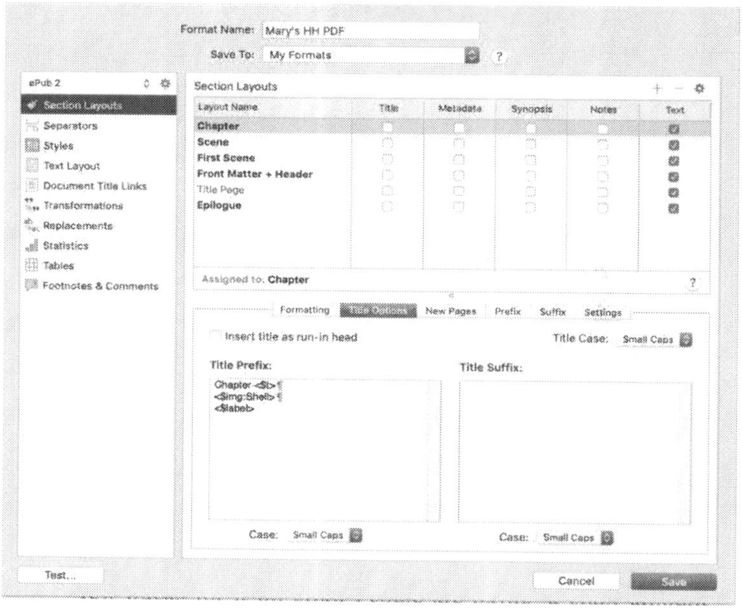

Figure 60: Modifying an Existing Format Within Scrivener 3

Users of earlier versions of Scrivener will recognize parts of this window. This is where you work with the nuts and bolts of how a Format is created.

Scrivener uses placeholders to make formatting changes. In the above example, I am using a placeholder to number my chapters to look like Chapter One. Because I have selected small caps, it looks more like CHAPTER ONE. Then, I have an image I use across my series. Lastly, because I alternate my character's point of view, I use labels to identify them and the label appears in the chapter heading.

The output of the placeholders used in the example above looks like this:

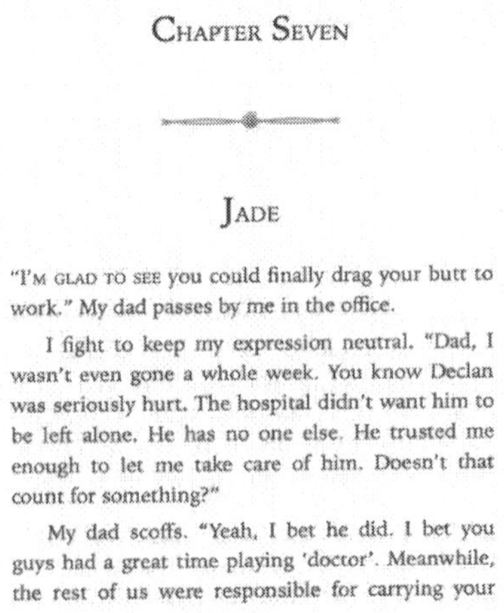

CHAPTER SEVEN

JADE

"I'M GLAD TO SEE you could finally drag your butt to work." My dad passes by me in the office.

I fight to keep my expression neutral. "Dad, I wasn't even gone a whole week. You know Declan was seriously hurt. The hospital didn't want him to be left alone. He has no one else. He trusted me enough to let me take care of him. Doesn't that count for something?"

My dad scoffs. "Yeah, I bet he did. I bet you guys had a great time playing 'doctor'. Meanwhile, the rest of us were responsible for carrying your

Figure 61: EPUB Output Using Placeholders in Scrivener 3

Although you don't have to, you can use placeholders in various parts of your document. In part, they are used to number things or identify things within your manuscript. Here are some of the more common placeholders to identify your chapters and sections.

<$n>	Inserts numbers like 1, 2, 3
<$sn>	Inserts numbers like 1,2,3 in sub documents.
<$w>	Inserts lowercase word for a number like one, two, three.
<$W>	Inserts uppercase word for the number like ONE, TWO, THREE.
<$t>	Inserts a title case word for number like One, Two, Three.
<$r>	Inserts lowercase Roman numbers i, ii, iii
<$R>	Inserts uppercase Roman numerals I, II, III
<$l>	Inserts lowercase letters for number like a, b, c
<$L>	Inserts lowercase letters for number like A, B, C

These placeholders can be used to label chapters or in section headings or to label page numbers.

You'll note that in several of my examples, I have an image placeholder. To use this, make sure the name of the graphics file in the research section of your Binder is the same as what you put in the placeholder. I use the same template for all of my fiction series regardless of the series. Each series has a different chapter heading graphic. So, after I drag my preferred image into the research section of the Binder, I simply rename it Shell. There's nothing magical about this name, it just happens to be the name of the file I used the first time I set this format up. It is easier for me to change the name of the graphic in my Binder than it is to adjust the placeholders.

There are many more placeholders available, for a list of them, consult the List of All Placeholders, located in the help section. This guide is quite comprehensive. Don't be overwhelmed. It is likely you'll only need a few of these placeholders.

To have Chapter 1 appear in your manuscript, you would place Chapter <n> under title options.

If you want to adjust the spacing and font size in the title you just created, go back to the formatting tab. You can change the font, font size, font color and line spacing. Title prefixes and suffixes can be formatted in different ways.

To add to the confusion, there are actually two tabs that say prefix and suffix. This is to add additional information. If you want to include a location or date, you could use these tabs. So, if your novel includes two locations, you could create a style type for each.

By clicking on New Page, you can set your options for your heading at the top of your page and whether you will be using small caps at the beginning of each chapter.

 If you have a blank line before the first line of text in your section, the small caps formatting will not show up.

The last tab is Settings. You can adjust how your indenting is handled based on the content of your document here.

You will have to set up each Section Layout separately. However, if you want to duplicate an existing section layout, click on the + after you have selected the section you would like to duplicate. Scrivener will place a new Section Type under the Section Layout you have selected. All the formatting will be carried over to the new Section Layout you have created. You can go in and make your changes to make it different from the one you just copied. Remember:

If you create a new Section Layout here, you need to go to Project Settings ⌥⌘, to add the Section Type so you can assign it to your files or documents.

Make sure you save your changes.

You can preview what your format will look like under the Section Layout Pane in the middle of the compiler page.

Now that you've applied your favorite format or created your own to apply to the files or documents you selected in the Compile Pane, now it's time to make sure Scrivener knows how to use those two types of information together. This is done in Section Layout Pane.

A Word About Separators

I would be remiss if I didn't touch on Separators. To access this menu go to Compile (⌥⌘E) and then right click on the format you want to work with. The separators menu is on the left-hand pane. Notice in the example below, .PDF is chosen. If you choose another type of output, different options will appear.

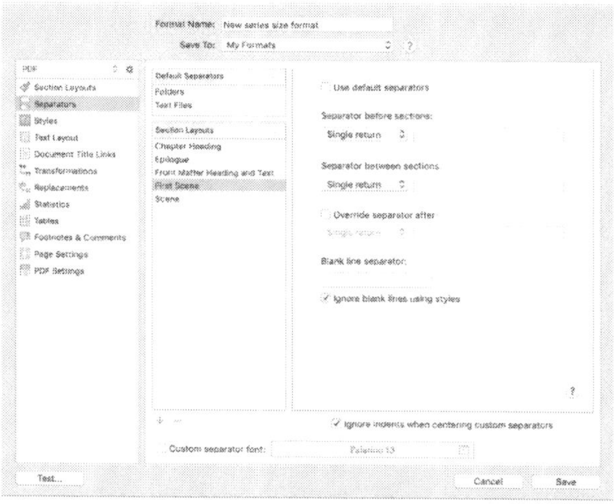

Figure 62: Setting Up Separators in Scrivener 3

Okay, it's time to own up to another one of my mistakes. Normally, I don't think much about separators in Scrivener. I have special Section Types set up for my first scene and the rest of my scenes with special formatting. I put an image on the top of the scene Section Type and usually everything works just fine.

Until it doesn't.

This is one of those situations where I need to give a huge shout-out to Bobby Treat for helping me understand why odd things were showing up in my table of contents.

I was taking a screenshot of a file I created using the new format I created for the relaunch of my series. I noticed the table of contents was terribly wonky. My sub-folders (which I name to make navigating around the quick search feature easier) were showing up in my table of contents. This was not what I wanted at all.

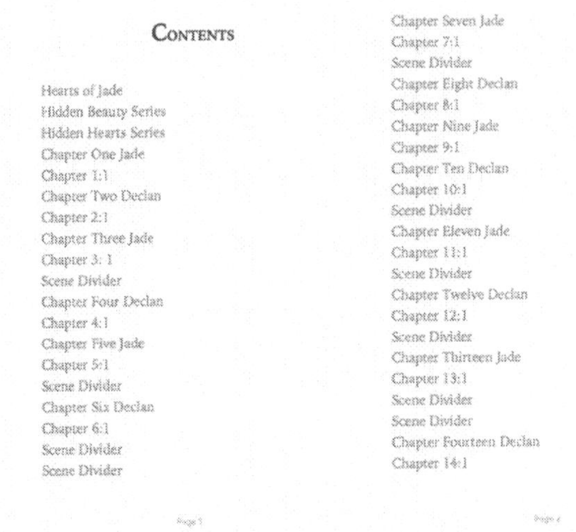

Contents

Figure 63: Separators Incorrectly Applied in Scrivener 3

I was very confused because when I created this new series format, I meticulously copied and pasted everything from an existing format which was working just fine. I double and triple checked to make sure everything was as it should be. The formats appeared to be identical. But, they weren't operating the same because I forgot to change some settings in Separators.

I learned the hard way that folders and documents are not treated exactly the same in Scrivener as I had always understood. The default separators are different. I like to work in folders. I don't know why. I guess maybe a folder looks more impressive than a piece of paper in my Binder – I'm weird that way.

Anyway, long story short (okay, short-ish), because I was using folders for my scenes and I had not changed the Separator settings, it was triggering an entry in the table of contents.

By default, folders have a page break set up as its default separator. This works okay if you're working with chapters. However, I was working with scenes within my chapters.

On the other hand, documents in Scrivener have an empty line as the default setting which does not trigger an entry into the table of contents or force a new page. Because of the way my manuscript is constructed, I needed to use a single return in my first scene and scene section layouts.

I left the page break as the default setting in my chapter, epilogue and front matter folders because I wanted a page break included. I also want these documents in my table contents.

If you want, you can also choose a wingding or webding to use in any blank spaces. There are already some default formats in Scrivener which use little graphics like this. If you want an example, the Modern Format uses them.

You need to set your separator preferences for each Section Type in your document.

Section Layout

The Section Layout Pane in the compiler is a new feature in Scrivener 3. Many people find this confusing. It doesn't have to be. Using my analogy of taking your manuscript to the print setter, you have now told the printer which documents you want in your book on the Compile Pane and identified which typeface, spacing and special formatting you want to apply in the Format Pane. Now, it's time to move on to the Section Layout Pane where you tell the printer which formatting you want to apply to each part of your manuscript.

When you first choose a Format for your document, if you have never used it with that particular project, you will encounter a window with a big yellow warning. This warning is to inform you that you need to assign section layouts. There is a button which says Assign Section Layouts.

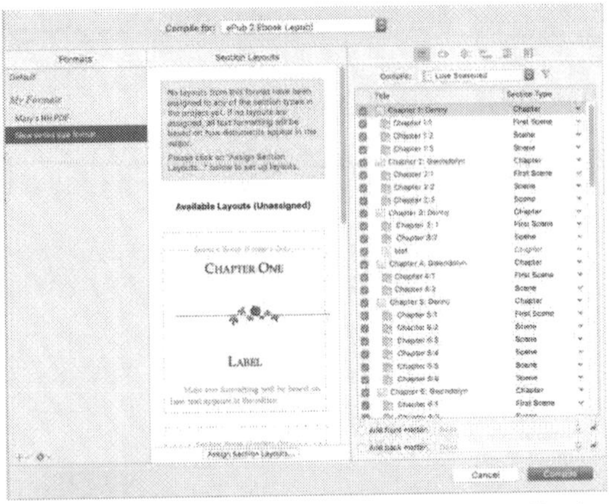

Figure 64: Assigning Section Layouts in Scrivener 3

When you click on this button, you will be presented with the Section Types you have used in your document. (If you wish to see more, you can click on a button to display the rest of your Section Types.) Next to that list, you will be shown the available Section Types for the format you have chosen. Now, it's a matter of matching them up.

You can either accomplish this by right clicking on a Section Type and choosing the Section Layout which corresponds with it from the drop-down list which appears or you can click on an individual Section Type and then click on the Format you want to use with it.

Final Steps of Compile

After you have accomplished this, you are ready to compile. The first thing that will happen when you click compile is that you will be asked to save your document somewhere. This is a matter of choice, but I have a folder for each title I'm working on and a folder for draft manuscripts.

At the bottom of the window, you'll have the opportunity to have Scrivener open an application to allow you to check the quality of the work. This is an optional step, but I always use it to make sure everything is as I intended it to be.

You can overwrite files with new files with the same name. However, I don't recommend this. Just choose an entirely different name. This will help avoid confusion when you upload your file for publication. I always date my files and if I'm working with multiple files during the day, I also add military time.

Congratulations! You've successfully created a document in Scrivener. Hopefully, it's everything you dreamed. But, sometimes it's not and working with outside programs might be helpful. I'm going to discuss some of those next.

Chapter 13 – Incorporating Scrivener into Your Workflow

Scrivener is a very powerful writing tool. It is comprehensive in nature. However, even Literature and Latte admits that the program is not designed to produce pristine finished work. Sometimes, it is helpful to use other programs in your workflow. This discussion will talk about some common options and how to efficiently work with outside people like beta readers and editors.

Personally, I use Scrivener 3 for almost everything. However, there are parts of the process of writing a book where I employ other programs such as Dragon® Professional Individual 6.0.8,

ProWritingAid, Photoshop and Microsoft Word. Sometimes, it takes a village to create a professional-looking manuscript. If you use other software resources while using Scrivener, it doesn't mean that you are a failure at Scrivener. The great thing about this program is that it enables you to use the part you feel comfortable with and that help you but doesn't require you to know and use every function.

Working with External Programs

I frequently tell people I use Scrivener to write and format all of my books. This is true … and false.

While I create, organize, write and format my books using Scrivener, Scrivener is not the only program I use. Because of the nature of my disability, I use Dragon® Professional Individual 6.0.8. I actually completely switched platforms because of Scrivener for Mac. Without voice recognition software, I could not write. It's as simple as that.

Dragon® is critical for my success, but it is not the only program I use to complete my manuscripts. I also perform my finish formatting in Microsoft Word, make chapter headings and title pages in Adobe Photoshop, and edit my work with ProWritingAid.

I don't work with Google Docs or Pages much, but I know other people do, so I will cover those.

Let's start with how I get words on the page.

Scrivener and Dragon®

Fortunately for me Dragon® Professional Individual 6.0.8 works exceptionally well with Scrivener 3. For those of you who are not users of voice recognition software, some of this discussion may not make much sense. But I'll try to give you an overview.

Dragon® Professional Individual 6.0.8 is – or was – a speech-to-text program offered by Nuance. Even though the Mac operating system offers speech-to-text abilities, they are not nearly as powerful as Dragon® Professional Individual 6.0.8. Unfortunately for all of us, Nuance stopped selling and supporting the Mac version on October 22, 2018.

If you own Dragon® Professional Individual 6.0.8, you can breathe a sigh of relief. It works fine with Mojave, and I have done a successful trial with the beta version of Catalina (Apple's new operating system).

If you don't own the Mac version of Dragon®, and you want to try it, as of October 2019, it is still available from Amazon, Best Buy, Newegg, TigerDirect and Walmart. If you purchase a copy of the program off of eBay, make sure the license is still new. Nuance has a habit of turning licenses off which they deem to have multiple users.

There are two ways to work with Dragon® and Scrivener 3. You can dictate directly into Scrivener or transcribe your files and import them into Scrivener. Each approach has its pros and cons, so I will discuss each briefly.

Direct Dictation

Part of the reason I use a Mac now is because I wanted the ability to dictate directly into Scrivener 3 with Dragon® without having to copy and paste. It works beautifully and I dictate thousands of words every day. I have full text control – meaning I can correct my mistakes within Scrivener. Unlike working in Microsoft Word, Dragon® does not seem to get bogged down by Scrivener.

To dictate fiction efficiently, I add my custom vocabulary words into Dragon® so I have to make fewer corrections. I typically dictate directly into Scrivenings. The compose mode works as well, but sometimes Dragon® gets a little lost when using compose mode and the cursor jumps around your document and can sometimes delete text randomly. Fortunately, if this happens, just press ⌘Z and say Cache Document and you'll be good to go.

Dragon® has one other glitch that could impact your work in Scrivener. It inserts extra spaces. To deal with this pesky issue, use project replace and type in two spaces in the Replace blank, and one space in the With blank. That should remove any extra spaces or, you can use the text tidying tool which has a setting to remove extra spaces. One place where Dragon® can add extra spaces is at the beginning of the paragraph. To delete those, highlight the paragraph mark and copy it. Then, paste it into the Replace blank in Project Replace and add a space after it. In the With blank, just put a plain paragraph mark. This will delete the space before paragraphs everywhere except for the very first paragraph in your folder or document. That one you will have to delete by hand.

Another option is Dragon® Anywhere. This is a subscription service from Nuance for a program which runs on both iOS and Android devices. It is not as full-featured as the desktop version of Dragon®. However, many people find it helpful for dictating on the move. Dragon® Anywhere requires Wi-Fi access.

I have used voice recognition software for thirty years. So, I am used to having the words appear in front of me on the screen. Therefore, I don't use transcription as much as I probably should. Many authors, including me, find that using transcription speeds up their dictation because they are not focused on correcting mistakes.

Transcription

Transcription is a great option for people who want to dictate away from their computer.

 Don't dictate while you drive.

I just have to get that out there. I know there are people who dictate while driving. However, as a former Disability Advocate, I have seen too many of my friends' lives destroyed by people who were driving distracted. I know we are all on deadlines, but please don't take the risk.

Even if you can't dictate while you're driving, there are many other places you can dictate for transcription. Many people do it while they take their dogs for a walk, wait for their kids to arrive in the pickup line at school, or even while they wait for an appointment.

Basically, transcription involves recording your voice and creating an audio file to upload to your computer so that a program like Dragon can turn it into text. Aside from Dragon, you'll need a recording device and a microphone.

You can either buy a small digital recorder with a USB card or, you can use your cell phone. Although I own two digital recorders, I prefer to use my cell phone.

Voice Record Pro is a program which records your speech and sends it directly to Dropbox, OneDrive, your email address or several other places. That makes it convenient to use with the transcription setting in Dragon®.

When you transcribe files, you can save them as .RTF files or Microsoft Word documents. If you use Microsoft Word documents, I suggest you import them into your Scrivener projects using Import and Split.

If you want more information on Dragon® or transcription, the first two books of the Empowering Productivity series are about voice recognition software and integrating it into your writing process.

Now that I've talked about getting my words on paper, now I'll talk about my favorite tool for editing, ProWritingAid.

Scrivener and ProWritingAid

I can't say enough positive things about ProWritingAid. I have a lifetime subscription to this grammar checking tool. I believe it has made me a stronger writer. One of my favorite things about this tool is that it works directly with your Scrivener file.

 If you want to open your project in ProWritingAid, make sure you have closed your Scrivener project first.

If you've failed to do so, ProWritingAid will give you a warning message. It is not a good idea to work with multiple copies of your project. It can get confusing quickly and put your words at risk. If you haven't used ProWritingAid in a while and were frustrated by ProWritingAid's tendency to recognize Scrivener's coding as mistakes, recent upgrades have taken care of that little glitch.

I'm a very consistent writer. I repeatedly make the same mistakes. While I am still in Scrivener, I eliminate words I commonly overuse. These include that, just, pretty, so, little bit, and going to. I review one chapter at a time and limit my search parameters to one or two chapters so the process doesn't become overwhelming. Doing this preemptive work saves me time in ProWritingAid. You may also want to remove any double spaces and make sure your quotation marks are consistent. ProWritingAid will mark them if one half of your quote is with straight quotes and the other half is curly.

When you start ProWritingAid, you can run a variety of checks on your document. I use the combo report and fix a bunch of things at once. Consequently, I run the checks on one chapter at a time.

 ProWritingAid can get bogged down if you do a grammar check on a large document all at once.

While open in ProWritingAid, your project will look different. That's okay. Don't panic, your formatting will still be there when you reopen your project in Scrivener.

After you've made your changes, make sure you save them. If the save option is grayed out, you need to make one more change in your document. It's kind of a glitch in ProWritingAid. Usually, I can find a comma or yet another instance of the word that to delete. After I've made that last correction, ProWritingAid allows me to save.

Close ProWritingAid before you try to open your document back up in Scrivener. All your changes will appear in your Scrivener project.

Again, if you are working with Dropbox, make sure your project is completely saved. Scrivener files can be large. It could take some time.

I've told you how I get words on the paper and how I make them the best they can be, now I'm going to describe how I incorporate Microsoft Word into my publishing process.

Scrivener and Microsoft Word

Let me start this section by acknowledging that it is entirely possible to produce a PDF using Scrivener alone. For the most part, things turn out just fine. However, I have had issues with mirrored margins and orphaned text. This is one reason I do my finish formatting with Microsoft Word. I adjust the margins by putting in a gutter and adjust any spacing abnormalities by hand.

The other reason I use Microsoft Word is because virtually every editor I have ever worked with prefers to use it over Scrivener. Since I write with my pages mostly formatted, I just finish the job up in Microsoft Word before I give my manuscript to my beta readers and editors.

This is where Scrivener really shines. Sometimes, my readers and my editor get my work a couple chapters at a time. Using compile, I can compile only the chapters I need to give them.

I give my beta readers and my editor Word documents to allow them to use track changes. Even though Scrivener has a helpful revisions mode, it still doesn't make the changes for you. In this area, Microsoft Word has Scrivener beat by a mile, in my opinion.

I treat my Scrivener project as my master manuscript. Therefore, after I have made my edits and the readers have given their feedback, I move my work from Microsoft Word back into Scrivener. Personally, I do it one chapter at a time. It just gives me one more chance to look at my words against a different background than I used in Microsoft Word. Sometimes, I find typos during this process.

However, if you don't want to copy and paste your chapters one at a time, you can use Import and Split just like you may have done when you started working with your document. Although some people have many copies of the manuscript in their Draft Folder, I recommend moving the old file to the Research Folder before performing the Import and Split function on your edited document.

The cleanup editing in Microsoft Word generally produces a beautiful document. However, I have an artistic streak a mile wide. So, I always have to dress it up a little. To do this, I use Adobe Photoshop. I also use Adobe Pro DC to produce my final PDF to upload to Amazon and Ingram Spark.

Scrivener and Adobe Photoshop

I've been known to make elaborate chapter headings for each character in my novels in addition to a title page. Even though I print my books in black and white, I still do my embellishments in color because more and more people are reading e-books on their cell phones and tablets which can display color files. These days, I don't create different chapter headings for each book because I want my series to look unified. However, I still use Photoshop to create my title pages.

MARY
CRAWFORD

Heart OF
Summers

HIDDEN BEAUTY BOOK 13

Figure 65: : Title Page Created in Adobe Photoshop and Inserted into Scrivener 3

This is one I created for my upcoming work-in-progress. It's pretty, but large files can increase your delivery cost. So, when I save my title pages, I use the Export function in Adobe Photoshop and tell it to Save for Legacy. This setting allows you to preserve the appearance while still shrinking the file size.

Then, to use it in Scrivener, I make a folder in my front matter and name it the same as the title of my book. After that, I click on Insert ▸ Image From File.

If you are planning to make a paperback, make sure your title page is three hundred dpi or better.

The other Adobe program I use is Adobe DC Pro. This allows me to export a proper .PDF compatible with Ingram Spark. First, I use the export .PDF function in Microsoft Word to create my .PDF. It is important that you set the proper page size and margins within Microsoft Word before you do this.

Then, after I have created the .PDF, I open it in Adobe DC Pro and run a preflight check on it. Preflight is located under the Edit menu or you can use ⇧⌘X. Ingram Spark prefers to use PDF/X - 1a files. Running your PDF through this one last step helps make sure there are no issues while you upload to Ingram Spark.

Although I don't routinely work with Google Docs or Pages, many people do, so I'm going to talk a little about working in those two programs with Scrivener.

Scrivener and Google Docs or Pages

Although I don't know very many people who write directly into Pages, it has some beautiful formatting options and if you upload your manuscript to Apple, Pages has a mechanism to do that directly.

Scrivener cannot import documents created in Pages directly. Therefore, you'll need to export it to another format first. You can export to .RTF or a Microsoft Word document. Pages does a superb job of converting to Word documents.

Once you have created a Word document, you

can use Import and Split to put it into folders in your Binder.

Interestingly, you can open Word documents in Pages and then save them as a Page document. So, if you want to take advantage of Apple's streamlined publishing process using Pages, you could compile a document from Scrivener into Microsoft Word and then convert that into a Pages document.

Google Docs is a favorite among authors, especially those like to work collaboratively. I can see why. Your files are available anywhere you have Internet access and multiple people can collaborate on them without risking any data.

Google Docs has a voice typing tool with some odd limitations. It is missing basic punctuation like quotation marks, colons and semicolons. If your characters tend to cuss, Google Docs Voice Typing may not be the tool for you. Cuss words are censored in Google Docs.

 Like Pages, Google Docs can work with Microsoft Word documents and output them as well.

To work with a document you created in Google Docs in Scrivener, you'll need to export it as a Microsoft Word document. To do so, save the file to your Google drive. Click on file then download. There will be another menu available. You can save your document as an .RTF, a text file or a Microsoft Word file. As before, you can use Import or Import and Split to bring the Microsoft Word document into Scrivener.

Unfortunately, there is no standard software for writing that everyone uses. However, most people who haven't discovered Scrivener yet use Microsoft Word. This includes your beta readers and editors. So, next I'm going to talk about how to incorporate working with other people who use other software into your writing process.

Working with Your Editor and Beta Readers.

Almost every beta reader and editor I've ever used prefers to work in Microsoft Word. I don't mind this because Microsoft Word has track changes which works far better than Scrivener's revision mode.

I try to vet beta readers carefully and I have a strong team now. However, every once in a while, I will get a new beta reader I haven't worked with before. In that case, I don't provide them with a Microsoft Word document. Instead, I issue a special .EPUB for them which I upload to BookFunnel. If they give me valuable feedback and want to continue being my beta reader, I move them up into my primary beta reading team. Those people get Microsoft Word documents directly from me.

Recent changes in Amazon's process means you don't actually have to upload a file when you post a preorder.

This policy change has made the process much easier for me. Now, once I have shared my book with my beta readers and editor, I don't put it back into Scrivener until after I have completed all the edits. (I used to do it after each round of feedback to make sure I had the most up-to-date manuscript available on Amazon for the preorder process.)

I work with the Microsoft Word document using track changes and, after I have completed all the edits, I copy and paste my Word document back into Scrivener one chapter at a time. It is entirely possible to use Import and Split for this function. However, I choose not to because pasting my document back in one chunk at a time allows me to take a last-minute look to find typos and continuity errors.

I use the Remove Small Caps feature under Edit ► Transformations to remove the small caps that I have imported from my Word document. Sometimes, you may have to reformat a paragraph that contains small caps and doing so can change the way they look. So, when it's back in my Scrivener file, I remove them to avoid this problem.

I always give my beta readers a final version of the book they've been working on to thank them for all their hard work.

If you are working with an editor or beta reader who gives you lots of comments, make sure you have deleted them all before you import your document back into Scrivener. I have seen them cause real havoc. It's easier to eliminate them in Microsoft Word.

When you are transferring your file back to Scrivener, use a slightly different text color in your editing window. That way, you will know which sections of your document you have already completed.

My process may not work for you; you need to adjust your workflow to whatever makes you comfortable.

Making the Process Work for You

I hang out on a lot of boards dedicated to the craft of writing and the subject of technology and how to properly use it comes up often. I'm always amazed when I read about everyone else's process because it's often different from mine. In this book, I have done my best to highlight things that worked well for me and caution you against the things that have not.

However, that doesn't mean you have to adopt my approach to using Scrivener. One of the great things about this program is that you can adapt it to the way you work. Some people only use Scrivener for the organizational features and write their documents in Microsoft Word. If that's what floats your boat, more power to you.

The goal is to make you as productive as you want to be. Scrivener can help with that, but don't feel like everyone's process has to be the same. My advice is to develop a workflow that works for you and adjust it as you learn new skills and grow as an author.

Next, I'm going to address some troubleshooting techniques for some common issues including how to restore your project from your backup, common compiling issues and how to work with Scrivener iOS with Scrivener 3 for Mac.

Chapter 14 – Troubleshooting

Restoring from Backup

Sometimes, despite our best efforts, things go wrong. Fortunately, Scrivener 3 has automatic backup settings. If you are concerned about the frequency of your backup files, you can backup manually by clicking on File ▸ Backup ▸ Backup Now.

Before automatic backing up can occur, you have to set it up in Preferences. (⌘,) Choose the Backup tab and set up a location and the behavior you want Scrivener to do when backing up. If you don't have issues with hard drive space, I recommend keeping more than just five backup files. If you don't use a program like Time Machine to back up your whole hard drive, I suggest you set this location somewhere on the cloud. Personally, I have my backup files saved in a different cloud service than I keep my active documents. I save my works in progress to Dropbox but my backup files on the iCloud.

If the catastrophic happens, first take a deep breath. Then go to Preferences. (⌘,) and choose the Backup tab. Click on Open Backup Location and a menu of your zipped backups will appear. Choose a backup file that was made before your problem started. Right click on the file and duplicate it.

Drag the copy of your file to your desktop or another file you have created in the Finder. Then click on it. You will find a .scriv file you can open. Although there are other types of files in the folder, the .scriv file is the only one you can open.

Most, if not all, of your words should be in that file. If you are still having difficulties, you might need to go to an earlier backup file.

If your project stops working and you need to restore it from a backup copy, I recommend calling the restored file something different from your original file in case the problem was created by a corrupted file.

You may be saying to yourself, "So, that sounds like a huge hassle. How do I stop my file from being corrupted?"

The most important thing you can do is to wait until your file is completely saved before you close the project in Scrivener. I know this seems simple, but as your file increases in size, it will take longer to save. Make sure you don't harm your project by being too inpatient.

 When you are using cloud services like Dropbox, make sure you have reliable Wi-Fi access.

My next tip may also seem intuitive, but sometimes people forget. Work with your laptop plugged in whenever possible. When your computer shuts down unexpectedly because your battery dies, awful things can happen to your work.

After I lost a substantial number of words because of a computer malfunction, I have become compulsive about creating backup copies. I have Time Machine set up to an 8 TB external drive. Twice a year, I backup all of my projects to a thumb drive just for safekeeping. If that were not enough, every day or every other day depending on how much I've written I compile a Microsoft Word document and send it to myself on Facebook. You don't have to be as obsessive as I am about creating backups, but losing fifteen thousand words has made me a little paranoid. I need to be clear that Scrivener was not at fault in my data loss, I had a problem with my hard drive which had not been diagnosed.

A corrupt file may not be the only thing you need to troubleshoot. Sometimes, compiling documents can be tricky. Next, we'll talk about some common issues which may create difficulties.

Common Compiling issues

You may have noticed there are a lot of moving parts in Scrivener and sometimes, things go awry. It can be discouraging when your hard-earned words don't turn out the way you want them to. But if you're having difficulties, I'll give you some tips to help.

Making Sure Your Ducks Are in a Row

In Scrivener 3, there are three areas you need to pay attention to. First, make sure all the documents you want to appear are checked in the compiler. This starts with the very first folder which contains your manuscript. Although it is possible to have more than one manuscript in your Draft Folder, I don't recommend it (unless you are creating an omnibus).

If your Binder contains duplicate folders, it can cause confusion and make it difficult to determine which one you are editing. If you have re-imported your corrected file after you have made corrections in an external program like Microsoft Word, move your old folders to your Research Folder. In fact, it's even better to create a folder called old manuscript and put the files in there.

Make sure you don't have a filter applied. I have personal experience with this, I had inadvertently set this filter to excluded files and then I was puzzled why my whole manuscript didn't compile. So, just keep an eye out to make sure you haven't inadvertently filtered out the files you want.

Next, take a moment to make sure all the documents or files you want in your final document are checked. Not surprisingly, I've also made this mistake. Imagine my humiliation when I discovered such a basic mistake. So, take a simple lesson from me and double check to make sure everything is included in your Compile Pane. This is a good time to confirm you have included everything.

Assigning Section Types to the wrong Section Layout when you assign them in the Section Layout Pane can skew your output. If that happens, just reassign them in the Compiler.

As I talked about earlier, if you are having trouble with your table of contents, make sure you examine the separator settings so that you don't inadvertently use a page break when you intend to use a single line or return. Page breaks trigger entries in your table contents.

Make sure you are using the correct placeholders when you set up your format options. A single letter can throw off your entire layout.

Text Color and Hyperlinks

Scrivener makes it wonderfully simple to be creative when you write. However, sometimes you may not want to share the extent of your creativity with everyone else. If you are like me and write with your text in a different color, you probably want your text to appear normal in your document when it is output. If so, you can check the box in the compiler to remove text color. This setting returns your text color to black (or white on a dark background).

Using hyperlinks in <u>Scrivener 3</u> is pretty easy. However, the way you access them is not intuitive. Instead of being on the insert menu, you can find hyperlinks under Edit ▸ Add Link. From here, it acts as a traditional hyperlink tool. To make the link above, I just highlighted the words Scrivener 3 and inserted a hyperlink to their website.

If you right-click on a hyperlink, you can edit it or remove it entirely. This is a handy feature because when you upload books to other platforms, they do not allow links directly to Amazon.

There may be times when you do not want hyperlinks to appear in your final document. You can have Scrivener remove the hyperlinks in your output by changing the setting under the gear in the Compile Pane.

Issues with Graphic Size

I recently encountered a problem with my format when I started another series and needed a different chapter heading graphic. For whatever reason, my new graphic wasn't displaying the same as my previous one. Once again Bobby Treat came up with a great solution. I want to share it with you in case you encounter the same difficulties.

If you need to adjust the size of your images in Scrivener 3, you can easily do so with placeholders. This is a two-step process. It's really helpful because you can resize your images based on the type of output you are using. For example, your image may look one way at 72 DPI for an e-book, but need to be resized when you output them at 300 DPI for your paperback. Scrivener allows you to adjust this easily.

The first step is to add a placeholder to your image in your format. ImageWidth is just a term to identify what we want replaced. You could use any term here. You will need to repeat these steps in every Section Layout in which you have an image you need adjusted.

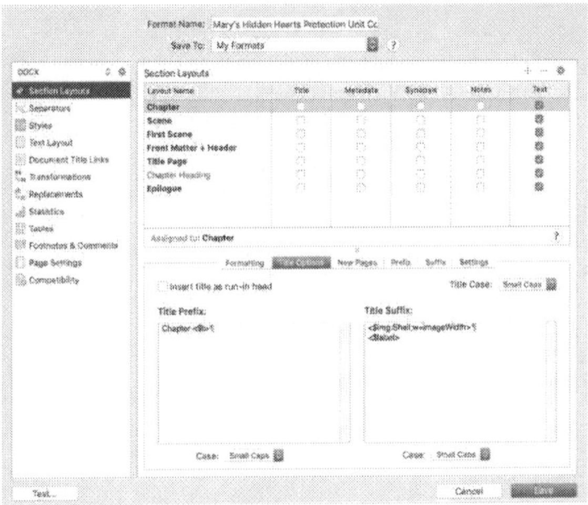

Figure 66: Adding Image Width as a Placeholder (Part 1)

The next step is to add the definition of image width into the replacement tool.

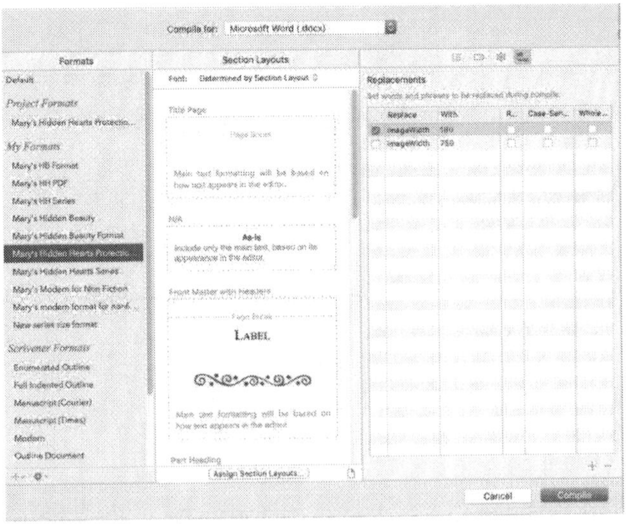

Figure 67: Adding Image Width as a Placeholder (Part 2)

In the example above, I defined the image width as 180 pixels for the e-book and 750 pixels for the paperback. After you've set your image width, you are ready to compile and create a beautiful book. You may have to play around to see which setting works best for your image. You can easily do this by adding more image widths to this replacement list and trying each one out individually. It works best to only check one box in this window.

If Section Types are not being assigned the way you expect them to be, make sure your folders are in the correct hierarchy in your Binder. If they are indented differently, the Section Type may not be applied properly. (This concept is similar to the levels feature in earlier versions of Scrivener.) It can be found under Project Settings.

Glitchy Formats

I'm not even sure what to call this or even if it needs its own section, however in case your formats suddenly stop working, I want to share with you my workaround or solution. I have encountered one anomaly that I haven't seen reported much. This is why I am so fanatic about backing up all my settings in Scrivener including my preferences and my formats.

After using a format for quite some time, it can appear to become degraded and leave out sections of your manuscript for no clear reason. I have found that deleting the offending format and importing a fresh copy helps eliminate this issue. Like I said, I'm not a computer programmer, so I'm not sure what is causing this to happen. I just have a practical solution.

As great as Scrivener 3 is on the Mac, sometimes you might want to go mobile. So, next I will briefly overview working with Scrivener for iOS.

Working with iOS Scrivener

Many Scrivener fans like to take their work mobile. Fortunately, Scrivener has developed an iOS version of their software. It is not as full-featured as the Mac version, but it gives you a way to work with your files in a familiar format and sync them back to your computer. For less than twenty dollars, this is an economical way to add writing tools to your workflow.

After you have purchased and downloaded your app from the Apple Store, the next thing you'll need is a Dropbox account. This is required to work with iOS syncing.

If you want to use the iOS version with your files, the default syncing path looks like this:

Dropbox ▸ apps ▸ Scrivener ▸ [project name]

You can change where Dropbox looks for your files by clicking on the edit button on the upper left-hand side of the app. After you do that, there is a gear down at the bottom left which will allow you to change your settings including your default Dropbox location.

If you have already synced some files to Scrivener from your old file location, the program will ask you if you want to keep those projects or discard them.

If you want to work with your existing files in your iOS version of Scrivener, you need to make sure your projects are copied into the folder on Dropbox where you told Scrivener iOS to look for them. You can do this via the Finder program on your Mac.

Make sure you are copying the whole Scrivener project. These will end in .SCRIV. Files that end in .XML are not full Scrivener projects and should not be moved separately.

If you plan to upload your projects to your iPad, make sure you have Wi-Fi access and plenty of time. Scrivener files can be quite large and take quite some time to upload to your iPad. I learned the hard way that you shouldn't try to do this on the road with limited Wi-Fi.

If you have several Scrivener projects, you may want to direct Scrivener to search for your work-in-progress in a file with very few other Scrivener projects. Having fewer projects to sync will help speed up the process. If you are having difficulty syncing your projects with the iOS version, double check your Wi-Fi connection and make sure it is functioning properly.

Most of the features of Scrivener for Mac are available for the iOS. For example, you have access to the Binder, your Inspector and a Scrivenings window. Additionally, you can work with your corkboard and Index cards as well as your labels and status.

You can also add a new project from scratch. Scrivener iOS allows you to add documents and folders just as the Mac version does.

If you have changed your project when you go back to the project list, there will be a blue triangle in your project. This symbol shows your project needs to be synced. You can set your iPad or iPhone to automatically sync Dropbox files in the settings or you can use the sync button on your device.

When you go back to your Mac, you can check to make sure the changes have been synced by clicking on File ▸ Sync ▸ Mobile Devices.

Do not use File ▸ Sync ▸ External Files the sync with iOS. This setting is intended to sync your files to outside files. This does not update your Scrivener iOS file. It is designed to export text files to an external file.

Although there is mixed advice on this topic, I recommend that you save and close your file on your Mac before trying to sync it with the iOS device. I have heard contrary advice which suggests that you can have both versions open at the same time. I have not found this to be the case.

To ensure your syncing process goes smoothly, make sure you have good Wi-Fi access and you wait until Dropbox is finished saving your file before you close it. Failure to do so can cause data loss.

Once you have uploaded your project to Scrivener iOS, you don't need Wi-Fi access to work on your file. You just need Wi-Fi access to sync your files.

If red icons appear on your project in iOS after you have synced it, try syncing it again. Sometimes it can take more than one try.

This was just an overview of working with Scrivener iOS. If you need more help, Literature and Latte has several tutorial videos on their site.

Chapter 15 – Wrap up and Random Thoughts

I just threw a huge load of information at you. I hope you find it helpful. If your head is reeling, I want to remind you that although Scrivener 3 is a powerful piece of software, you need not learn all of it at once. You can learn the pieces you use most often and then supplement your knowledge as you go along.

Having said that, one of the best ways to learn Scrivener is just to dive in and experiment. If experimenting is terrifying to you, you can always make a test copy of your work in Finder and leave the original copy untouched.

Scrivener is a phenomenally powerful program with the ability to do countless things to help you become a better writer. I tried to cover the features I use most often or find potentially helpful. As with everything else, your mileage may vary. Your writing process may look very different from mine and that's okay.

Some of you may be asking yourself why I didn't cover Scrivener 3 for Windows. At the moment, Scrivener 3 for Windows is not available because programmers at Literature and Latte are still working out the bugs. We remain ever hopeful that the release of Scrivener 3 for Windows is imminent. I am working on An Everyday Guide to Scrivener 3 for Windows to address your questions and concerns when that day comes.

I also have written two other books in the Empowering Productivity series which deal with effectively using dictation as an author.

In the meantime, if you have questions or comments, please email me at Mary@MaryCrawfordAuthor.com or find me on the following social networks:

Facebook: www.facebook.com/authormarycrawford
Website: MaryCrawfordAuthor.com
Twitter: www.twitter.com/MaryCrawfordAut

Acknowledgements

I am blessed to have a great team around me. My three Kathys went above and beyond.

Kathy F. may never want to volunteer to help me again after sorting through copious amounts of keyboard shortcuts to verify they actually exist.

Kathern W. is game to read anything I write, even when it isn't a mushy romance novel. For that, I am eternally grateful. Thank you for being my constant cheerleader (even when you don't quite understand my plan).

Put quite simply, Kathy from Covers Unbound takes my plain, disjointed words and makes them beautiful. Her covers and formatting are amazing, and she did a masterful job steering me in the right direction when I had no idea what I was doing. It's a pleasure to work with you.

Lisa Lee — my editor extraordinaire. I admire your grit and tenacity to work under difficult circumstances and still cope with anything I throw at you. Thank you for making sense of my ramblings, so other people can learn something.

Lacie Redding, thank you for helping to make sure people know I actually write books. Your never-ending support is more helpful than you can imagine.

Thank you to David Lee Martin, Bobby Treat, Gwen Hernandez, and Karen Price for allowing me to join your Scrivener support community and soak up knowledge over the years. You guys have made me better at my job.

I went to give a special shout out to my husband, Leonard Crawford. I can't tell you how much I appreciate your help and support. Your insightful questions and suggestions helped me create a much stronger book. Thank you for always being in my corner.

To my son, Justin — I am so proud of the man you are becoming. Thank you for taking such great care of me when sometimes I'm too busy to take care of myself. I know you're busy succeeding like a boss in high school so, I understand that helping me can sometimes be a pain. Thanks for doing it anyway.

Resources

Retailers and Equipment:

Literature and Latte
https://www.literatureandlatte.com/ —
Scrivener is their signature program (although
they do make Scrapple). It is my go-to writing
program. I own three versions of it.

Nuance® ((Nuance.com) — the software company
which develops and supports Dragon® Dictate,
Dragon® NaturallySpeaking, and Dragon®
Anywhere.

KnowBrainer (Knowbrainer.com) — a software and
adaptive equipment online retailer with
comprehensive resources and an active forum
and helpful equipment guides.

Blue Mic (https://www.bluedesigns.com) — The
manufacturer of Yeti, Snowball, Raspberry
microphones (among others). These are
among the best microphones I've ever used for
voice recognition software.

Krisp (https://krisp.ai/) — This program creates a
virtual microphone which screens out and
necessary background noise.

Internet Communities:

Scrivener Users
https://www.facebook.com/groups/463927253627
424/ A very active Facebook group dedicated
to users of Scrivener. Beginners and experts

both post in this group. It is a great way to get your questions answered.

Scrivener Mac Heads
https://www.facebook.com/groups/174503729243 2636A Facebook group dedicated to helping the users of Scrivener 3 for Mac. Unlike the Scrivener users board, this one is focused on Scrivener 3 for Mac.

Dragon® Riders
https://www.facebook.com/groups/164813424544 2422 – This forum, which covers both versions of Dragon® Professional Individual is the most active group on Facebook. There are many participants who are well-versed in both programs and generous with their advice.

Dragon® NaturallySpeaking Users
https://www.facebook.com/groups/164813424544 2422– This group is also a Facebook group, but it's focus tends to be tailored toward NaturallySpeaking.

Additional Software, Courses and Books:

David Lee Martin – the most helpful Scrivener tutorials I've ever encountered. David also has helpful books. https://scrivener-unleashed.teachery.co/scrivener-unleashed

Gwen Hernandez – helpful Scrivener interactive tutorials and author of Scrivener for Dummies. http://gwenhernandez.com/

Karen Price – helpful Scrivener tutorial on Udemy
https://www.udemy.com/course/scrivener-3-full-course-on-how-to-use-scrivener

Grammarly (Grammarly.com) – A web-based grammar checking program. They offer both free and paid versions. Aside from Scrivener, this is my favorite place to dictate.

ProWritingAid (https://prowritingaid.com) – a fee-based grammar checking program. You can buy a lifetime subscription. This program works directly with Scrivener.

Tomato One
https://apps.apple.com/us/app/tomato-one-free-focus-timer– A flexible Pomodoro timer which allows you to set the amount of time you would like to write and the length of time you rest. It tracks the number of Pomodoro sessions you have completed each day.

Focus (Heyfocus.com) – a web blocking app for the Mac which allows you to use Pomodoro timers and customize the websites you block.

Focus Me (https://focusme.com/) Focus me is an app designed to block websites and increase your productivity. It is available for both Windows and Mac.

Pacemaker Press (https://www.pacemaker.press) – One of the ways I stay motivated is to track my progress. My favorite way to do this is with Pacemaker Press. I can track multiple projects and plan out my year.

Romancing the Beat: Story Structure for Romance Novels
http://gwenhayes.com/books/romancing-the-beat/, Gwen Hayes has created one of the most straightforward guides to writing romance novels I've ever seen. Even better, she has a Scrivener template based on the book available on her website.

The 8-Minute Writing Habit for Novelists: Triple Your Writing Speed and Learn Dictation to Produce More Words, Faster by Monica Leonelle, (https://theworldneedsyourbook.com/dictationresouces) – This book incorporates dictation into an overall strategy of writing faster. Dictation is just one component of a mindset of increasing your productivity.

Sprinting Groups and Other Resources:
Grotto Garden (https://www.facebook.com/groups/GrottoGarden/– Need a sprinting partner any time, day or night? Not a problem with this friendly group of folks. Just hop on and introduce yourself. The group is large enough that there are usually sprints happening around the clock.

NaNoWriMo (http://nanowrimo.org/) – Why not join us for National Novel Writing Month? Not only is it a fun challenge, you'll meet lots of other great writers and find a website chock full of great writing tips and prompts. It's also a great way to practice sprinting and earn discounts on software and editing programs – including Scrivener.

My Write Club (http://www.mywriteclub.com) – This is a great little motivating sprinting site. I love this site because it is so flexible. You can join a group sprint which is a group of random people. They have twenty-five minute sprints at the top and bottom of every hour. You can race against a group of people. You earn stars along the way for your progress which is incredibly motivating. You can also set up your own private sprint by yourself or with a group of friends. You can track your progress toward your goal.

About the Author

I have been lucky enough to live my own version of a romance novel. I married the guy who kissed me at summer camp. He told me on the night we met that he was going to marry me and be the father of my children.

Eventually, I stopped giggling when he said it, and we've been married for more than thirty years. We have two children. The oldest is a Doctor of Osteopathy. He is across the United States completing his residency, but when he's done, he is going to come back to Oregon and practice Family Medicine. Our youngest son is now tackling high school, where he is an honor student. He is interested in becoming an EMT.

I write full time now. I have published more than thirty books and have several more underway. I volunteer my time to a variety of causes. I have worked as a Civil Rights Attorney and Diversity Advocate. I spent several years working for various social service agencies before becoming an attorney.

In my spare time, I love to cook, decorate cakes and, of course, I obsessively, compulsively read.

I would be honored if you would take a few moments out of your busy day to check out my website, MaryCrawfordAuthor.com. While you're there, you can sign up for my newsletter and get a free book. I will be announcing my upcoming books and giving sneak peeks as well as sponsoring giveaways and giving you information about other interesting events.

If you have questions or comments, please E-mail me at Mary@MaryCrawfordAuthor.com or find me on the following social networks:

Facebook:
www.facebook.com/authormarycrawford

Website:
MaryCrawfordAuthor.com

Twitter:
www.twitter.com/MaryCrawfordAut

Books by Mary Crawford

Hidden Beauty Series

Until the Stars Fall from the Sky
So the Heart Can Dance
Joy and Tiers
Love Naturally
Love Seasoned
Love Claimed
If You Knew Me (and other silent musings) (novella)
Jude's Song
The Price of Freedom (novella)
Paths Not Taken
Dreams Change (novella)
Heart Wish (100% charity release)
Tempting Fate
The Letter
The Power of Will

Hidden Hearts Series

Identity of the Heart
Sheltered Hearts
Hearts of Jade
Port in the Storm (novella)
Love is More Than Skin Deep
Tough
Rectify
Pieces (a crossover novel)

Hearts Set Free
Freedom (a crossover novel)
The Long Road to Love (novella)

Hidden Hearts – Protection Unit

Love and Injustice
Out of Thin Air
Soul Scars

Empowering Productivity

The Power of Dictation
Use Your Voice
An Everyday Guide to Scrivener 3 for Mac
An Everyday Guide to Scrivener 3 for Windows

Other Works

Vision of the Heart
#AmWriting: A Collection of Letters to Benefit The
Wayne Foundation

Index

The Power of Dictation

Pro Tips for Authors: Make Dragon® Work for You

Wish your words could magically appear?

You are not alone.

What if I told you your wish is within reach? Dictation isn't magic, but it can seem like it. However, it can be daunting, overwhelming, and downright confusing. I've been using voice recognition software for thirty years and written over thirty books using both Dragon® Dictate for Mac and various versions of Dragon® NaturallySpeaking. n this updated and expanded version of *The Power of Dictation*, I demystify the world of voice recognition software for you.

7. Learn how to choose the right computer, microphone, and software for your needs.

8. This book covers the latest releases from Nuance, including Dragon® Professional Individual for Mac 6.0.8 (Dragon® Dictate) and Dragon® Professional Individual 15.3 for Windows (Dragon® NaturallySpeaking), and discusses how they stack up against other alternatives.

9. If you are a Mac user, learn how to get the most out of Dragon® Dictate without having to use an alternative operating system on your Mac.
10. Explore positive ways to make the transition from using your keyboard to using your voice to tell stories. • Discover how to increase your efficiency and productivity as you dictate.
11. Learn how to take your dictation mobile through the use of transcription.

Unlock the power of dictation and take your writing to a whole new level.

For more information visit:
http://marycrawfordauthor.com/project/the-power-of-dictation/

EMPOWERING PRODUCTIVITY - BOOK 2

❧ USE ❧
YOUR VOICE
The Art
of
Storytelling
with
Dictation

MARY CRAWFORD

Use Your Voice
The Art of Storytelling with Dictation

Does using dictation make your muse run in the other direction?

Voice recognition software is a powerful tool, yet some authors find it challenging to incorporate dictation into their writing style.

Use Your Voice is a comprehensive how-to-guide designed to help you integrate dictation into your writing process regardless of whether you are a plotter, a pantser, or a planser.

This book will help you choose the software and equipment that best meets your needs. It includes an overview of popular writing software and how those programs interact with dictation software.

Each writing style presents its own unique challenges when supported by dictation. Learn how to effectively incorporate dictation into the writing style which works best for you.

Turn your voice into your most powerful writing tool.

For more information visit:
https://marycrawfordauthor.com/project/use-your-voice/

Empowering Productivity Series

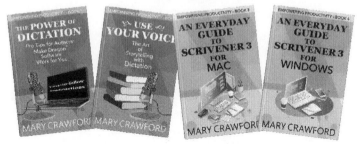

(Available in eBook & Paperback)

http://marycrawfordauthor.com/project/the-power-of-dictation/

http://marycrawfordauthor.com/project/use-your-voice/

❧❦

An Everyday Guide to Scrivener 3 for Mac and *An Everyday Guide to Scrivener 3* for Windows will be available soon. These guides will help you become familiar with the program and become comfortable — even if you are not a computer programmer.

https://marycrawfordauthor.com/project/an-everyday-guide-to-scrivener-3-for-mac/

https://marycrawfordauthor.com/project/an-everyday-guide-to-scrivener-3-for-windows/